Blen

BRADFORD ON AVON: PAST AND P

Cover: view of Tory by Jeremy Haslam

Bradford on Avon: a view from the east, 1988

BRADFORD ON AVON PAST AND PRESENT

Harold Fassnidge

Photography by Adam Tegetmeier

EX LIBRIS PRESS

First published in 1988 by
Ex Libris Press
1 The Shambles
Bradford on Avon
Wiltshire

Cover by 46 Design, Bradford on Avon
Typeset in 11 on 13 Plantin by
Saxon Printing Ltd., Derby
Printed in Great Britain by A. Wheaton & Co. Ltd, Exeter

ISBN 0 948578 09 2

CONTENTS

ACKNOWLEDGMENTS

My grateful thanks go to the staff of the Wiltshire Record Office, of the Local Studies Section of the Wiltshire Library and Museum Service and of the library of the Wiltshire Archaeological and Natural History Society, who could not have been more helpful, and also to the following who have helped in various ways: Mrs Mollie Dotesio, John Fassnidge of the National Army Museum, Mrs Barbara Harvey, Alan Hicks, Colin Johns of Wilts County Council, Roger Mawby, John Sargant, Vicar of Christ Church, Mrs Pamela Slocombe, Mrs Gillian Spriggs of Bradford on Avon Preservation Trust, Malcolm Thomas, Librarian of the Religious Society of Friends, and Miss Joan Uncles.

I have also drawn upon the following unpublished material kindly made available to me:

Christopher Moody's *History of Leigh Park Hotel*
Ivor Slocombe's *The Christ Church Schools*
Matthew Slocombe's university dissertation (1987), *Clothiers to Gentlemen: the development of the Yerbury family and the Belcombe estate at Bradford on Avon, Wilts.*
John C Shehan's *History of the Bradford on Avon Town Club*

PREFACE

As one of the team of honorary guides for Bradford on Avon Preservation Trust I have over a number of years had the pleasure of conducting parties of visitors around the town, not all of them from Britain, not all having much knowledge of our national history or of where local history fits into the pattern. In putting together this account I have borne in mind the questions I have been asked at various times by non-historian visitors and have assumed that the reader will have no great knowledge of English history, political or social. My intention therefore has been to present an accurate up-to-date picture of this attractive small town and its past mainly for the general reader. But I hope that the dedicated local historian also will find something of value.

Harold Fassnidge
Bradford on Avon
May 1988

About the author

Harold Fassnidge is a barrister who spent most of his working life in the Diplomatic Service. He fell in love with Bradford on Avon many years ago when on home leave from India and on retirement went there to live. He co-edited *Bradford on Avon: A Pictorial Record* (published in 1983 by Wiltshire Library and Museum Service) and in 1986 his monograph *The Quakers of Melksham* was awarded first prize in the Lloyd's Bank/County Council 1985/6 Wiltshire History Competition.

INTRODUCTION

Bradford on Avon begins where the Cotswolds end. It lies at the most southerly tip, a semi-circular escarpment reaching steeply southwards to the valley below. From riverside up to ancient Budbury a charming medley of stone houses and cottages of almost every style covers the slopes. On Newtown, Middle Rank and Tory tiers of houses form a kind of grandstand, from which to see, and be seen by, those in the valley below in mutual agreeable contemplation. Down by where the town bridge now stands (and where, a millennium and more ago, Saxon Bradford began) Saxon ox-wagons once crossed and re-crossed the broad ford which gave the town its name, and lumbering up the hillsides beyond created the winding ways we call now Silver Street and St Margaret's Street.

In 1913 the poet Edward Thomas, cycling through, paused to enjoy the scene:

> I dismounted by the empty Lamb Inn, with a statue of a black-faced lamb over its porch, and sat on the bridge. The Avon ran swift but calm and dull, down under the bridge and away westward. The town hill rises from off the water, covered as with scales with stone houses of countless varieties of blackened grey and many gables, and so steep that the roofs of one horizontal street are only just higher than the doorsteps of the one above. A brewery towers from the mass at the far side and, near the top, a factory with the words FOR SALE printed on the roof in huge letters. And the smoke of factories blew across the town. The hilltop above the houses is crested with beeches and rooks' nests against the blue. The narrow space between the foot of the hill and the river is occupied by private gardens, a church and its churchyard yews and chestnuts and by a tall empty factory based on the river bank itself, with a notice TO LET.

From *In Pursuit of Spring*, re-published in 1981 by Wildwood House Ltd.

BRADFORD ON AVON PAST AND PRESENT

Three quarters of a century later the scene is not greatly changed. The Lamb Inn has gone, and in its place stands part of the Avon Industrial Polymers complex of buildings. The houses are, for the most part, not nearly so blackened. The towering brewery in Newtown has closed long since, the building it occupied still prominent but rivalled now by the Rope Walk development. The tall factory (Abbey Mill), relic of the dead clothing industry, is still there, but has not been unoccupied since 1915 when it was taken over for rubber manufacture; it, too, is part of the Avon Industrial Polymers operation, used by them as a training centre and offices and for the manufacture of gaskets for aerosols. No longer does the smoke of factories blow across the town, though, smokeless, the town still largely earns its own living and preserves something of the atmosphere of the major manufacturing town it once was.

And the town *was* important, a leader in the clothing industry. From the earliest times good quality wool had always been abundant, producing income and clothing for rich and poor alike. From the fourteenth century (when the English, helped by a medieval brain-drain from Flanders, first learnt to spin and weave their own wool for sale as good quality finished cloth instead of sending it abroad for processing) up to the eighteenth century, Bradfordians, for the most part, prospered and some of them got very rich.

Like every other town and village Bradford on Avon streets were once filthy with garbage and ordure from man and beast. On at least two occasions that we know of, in 1609 and 1646, the town was afflicted with the plague, so sorely (for twenty long weeks on the earlier occasion) that towns and villages as far away as Chippenham had to be specially taxed to help out. Today's visitor, happily, does not need the reassurance offered in local directories in the eighteenth and nineteenth centuries that the town's situation was such that all impurities after passing down its sloping streets, were immediately carried off by the waters of the Avon...

Bradford on Avon was largely spared the spate of destruction which took place elsewhere in the name of progress in the 1960s, and since then the greater part of the town has been designated a conservation area. So, for the foreseeable future, Bradford's nooks and crannies, alleys and back-streets and above all its lovely old buildings, with their occasional little surprises, will continue to charm us all. Long may it be so!

1   CELTS, SAXONS ROMANS AND NORMANS

The Beginning

We know that in the Iron Age (roughly the thousand years before the birth of Christ) the high ground on the north side of the town (Budbury) was inhabited. What had previously been thought to be a prehistoric religious site, barrow or burial ground was found in 1969 to be the remains of an Iron Age fort. Excavation showed the defences to consist of a bank with double ditches in front. Iron Age pottery and other objects were found.

There was a Roman or Romano-British settlement on the same spot and to the north-west of it but it must have been small. The area was heavily wooded and well off the paved road which ran through Cunetio (Mildenhall) and Verlucio (Sandy Lane) to Aquae Sulis (Bath). The Roman settlers probably came by way of Bath, which was an important Roman town from the first century on. It would be natural for them to stay on the Bath side and in the same location as their Iron Age predecessors where the commanding views of the territory to the south will have impressed them. Until it was built on in 1986, what used to be called Bed and Bolster Field and is now called Budbury Ridge, retained the vestiges of what appeared to be a typical Roman *vallum* (rampart). Many Roman coins and fragments of other artefacts have been found in the area.

In Bath, as elsewhere, the senior ranks both military and civilian will have been Rome-based and patrician, the lower ones locally recruited. Who or what the first Roman or Romano-British residents of Bradford on Avon were we can only surmise from such archaeological evidence as

11

has become available. This evidence reveals a high degree of sophistica-
tion, particularly in the third century AD. But whether they were
thoroughly Romanised Britons or of Roman descent through intermarriage or a mixed community of both is uncertain.

In 1976 the remains of a Romano-British house of some quality were
discovered at Budbury. A dig[1] led by Alison Borthwick of the
Archaeological Section of Wiltshire County Council yielded evidence of
construction between the second and fourth centuries. A coin of AD 70
(Vespasian) was found at the lowest level excavated and post-holes near
by suggested occupation about that date. In its heyday, perhaps the
third century AD to judge by fragments of glass, painted plaster and
household equipment found at the higher levels and the existence of a
bath-house, it was the home of a prosperous landowner. Later it fell on
evil times, seemingly given over to use for grain-drying and storage and
at one point suffering fire damage. Of the many Roman coins found in
the Budbury area, the latest is of the time of the emperor Valens (AD
364-378). But if the Romans gave the settlement a name it has not come
down to us. What we do have from those days is the name of the river:
the word Avon derives from the Old British *abona* from which modern
Welsh derives *afon*.

A Truly Saxon Town

It was the Saxons who founded and named the town; and of the many
English Bradfords Bradford on Avon, with seniority from AD 652,
takes pride of place in the records. (The Yorkshire Bradford first
appears in 1086, some four centuries later, when William the Conqueror's diligent surveyors and enumerators recorded it in the Domesday Book). More than 13 centuries ago a battle was fought here. The
Anglo-Saxon Chronicle records that in AD 652 Cenwalh, king of
Wessex, fought at *Bradenforda be afne* (literally the broad ford on the
river). It may well be that the battle was where the town bridge now
stands. From time immemorial this has been the site of a ford and,
indeed, it continued to be used as such until the present embankments
were created. Kelly's Directories up to 1900 stated that the river could
be crossed dryshod here.

What gave rise to the dispute or against whom Cenwalh was fighting is
uncertain because the chroniclers do not agree. But less than a century
before (until the Saxon victory at Dyrham in AD 577) the town had been
within British (Welsh) territory, a short distance beyond the north-west

Here, most probably, was the broad ford on the Avon which, thirteen centuries ago, gave the town its name. The river was fordable at this point up to the beginning of the present century.

frontier of Wessex. To the north and west dispossessed Welshmen will have nursed resentment. What the Saxons had taken from them had been quite literally the land of their fathers and reprisals will doubtless have been attempted from time to time; so it seems likely that it was against them for control of the river, a natural frontier and highway.

The earliest Saxon settlement will have been on the south side of the river and its broad ford, probably occupying the high ground of what is now St Margaret's Hill, St Margaret's Place and St Margaret's Villas. Once the river was securely under their control the Saxons could cross over to the other bank and settle there. According to tradition the monastery or abbey known to have been established in Saxon times was located on the north bank roughly where the church of the Holy Trinity was later built. The names of Abbey House and Abbey Mills, built near what was once called Abbey Yard, remind us of this tradition.

Precisely when the West Saxons built their little church (of which more later) and how much the present building owes to the original one is uncertain, and the question has been the subject of much learned discussion. Best opinion seems to be that it was rebuilt in the reign of Aethelred II (978-1016) (Aethelred the Unredy), perhaps because the original structure had, Saxon-fashion, been made of wood and was by then crumbling away. But we do know from what William of Malmesbury wrote in 1125 that *it was said* to have been built by Bishop Aldhelm. Aldhelm, (c 640-709), a Benedictine monk of royal descent who subsequently became the first bishop of Sherborne, was almost certainly the founder of the monastery, of which he was abbot, and it may be that a church was erected near by to encourage the laity. (Christianity was still a novelty to Saxons with King Cenwalh himself only a recent convert).

The little church retains to this day one direct link with its founder. When Aldhelm died on a visit to Doulting, some 20 miles to the south-west, his body was carried back to his old home, the abbey at Malmesbury. By order of Ecquin, Bishop of Worcester, stone crosses were set up at the seven resting places on the way, of which Bradford on Avon was one; and what remains of the Bradford cross – two pieces – may be seen over the altar.

In 1988, the year of the millennium of the death of St Dunstan (c 909-988), it is appropriate to recall that both he and his enemy King Aethelred are part of Bradford's history. It was at an assembly here in the year 954 that under Eadred, King of Wessex, whose chief adviser he

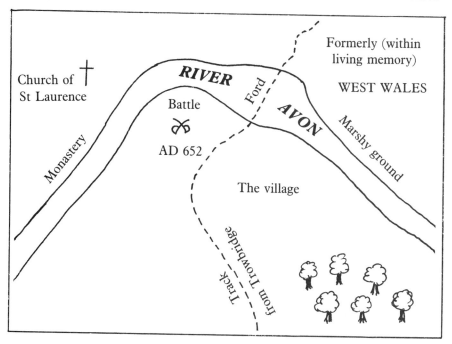

Bradford on Avon in Bishop Aldhelm's lifetime (AD 640-709).

was, Dunstan was made Bishop of Worcester. In due course (in 959) he became Archbishop of Canterbury[2] under his friend and ally King Edgar (959-975). Dunstan was as much politician as priest and when Edgar died in 975 he it was who settled the question of succession by arbitrarily crowning Edgar's son Edward ("the Martyr") in preference to Aethelred ("the Unredy"), his half-brother, thus incurring Aethelred's undying enmity. Three years later Edward was murdered at Corfe Castle at the instigation of Aethelred's mother Elfrida so that Aethelred could take his place on the throne.

With Aethelred king, Dunstan's political power was over. But perhaps his moral influence survived, even after his death in 988. The Manor of Bradford, comprising the monastery, the town and the neighbouring villages, was royal property. Troubled in conscience about how he had come to the throne, in the year 1001 Aethelred gave it to the Abbey of Shaftesbury "as a safe refuge for the nuns against the insults of the Danes, and a hiding place also for the relics of the blessed martyr St. Edward and the rest of the saints." In the event the monastery was sacked and totally destroyed soon afterwards, most probably by

15

BRADFORD ON AVON PAST AND PRESENT

Aethelred's old adversary Canute, who, as we know from the Anglo-Saxon Chronicles, raided up the river Frome in 1015. If Aethelred was sincere it seems odd that the abbey at Bradford on, or very near the bank of a river, should be thought safer than the one at Shaftesbury; perched as it was on very high ground the latter was surely much less vulnerable. Was this yet another misjudgement of the kind that earned Aethelred his Saxon nickname *Unredy* – the Ill-advised? Or did he secretly hope that by putting Edward's bones out of sight in remote Bradford he would thereby put them out of mind?

The Norman Heritage

The Norman Conquest created no great upheaval in Bradford. The Abbey of Shaftesbury continued to hold the manor of Bradford (42 hides – about 5,000 acres) and it would appear from the Domesday Book that at least some Anglo-Saxon landowners transferred their allegiance to William.

By the middle of the twelfth century the Normans built a larger church (now Holy Trinity) alongside the little Saxon one. Some of its Norman features remain.

To the Normans we also owe the town bridge, which, much repaired and restored over the centuries, nevertheless retains two late Norman (thirteenth century) arches; they are the ones nearest the south bank. The bridge as it is today is really two bridges in the sense that its width was doubled by the building alongside of another one in the latter half of the seventeenth century, a time of great prosperity in the town. If there was a bridge before the Normans came it was probably a wooden one – a "tree-bridge" like the one which gave neighbouring Trowbridge its name. But the Saxons may well have been content to splash bridgeless across the ford. Before the embankments were constructed around the turn of the present century horse-drawn vehicles could, and often did, use the ford for preference. An engraving of 1830 from a drawing by W Westall shows the unembanked slopes which made this possible.

Right up to the time of the widening of the bridge reluctance to spend money on it was a recurring problem and this reluctance is documented back to 1400 (when the Pope himself intervened); so the ford was doubtless seen from time to time as safer. Like fourteenth century Barton bridge leading to and from Barton Farm and the tithe barn it seems to have been built without parapets; and that from time to time a citizen took a tumble over the edge into the river we gather from a

16

minute of 1502 calling for a "copying" the lack of which was "to the grave danger of the King's people".

The population of the manor of Bradford at the time of the Norman Conquest was, according to Canon Jones, about 700, of whom some three to four hundred lived in the town itself. He based his calculation on the Domesday record; the population included (in descending order of social status) 33 *burgesses* (town dwellers), 40 *bordarii* (husbandmen or cottagers with holdings of, say, 15 to 20 acres), 22 hog-keepers, 18 *coliberti* (freedmen who continued to owe service) 36 *villani* (villagers, unfree, being owned by their feudal lord, unable to own land but allowed to farm it for themselves) and nine *serfs* (bondmen owned by their feudal lord). There were two mills and a market. There was also a vineyard of about an acre (one arpen).

The only king known to have visited Bradford was a Norman one, the egregious King John (1199-1216) who found himself here in August 1216 in the course of his armed struggle with the barons who a year before had forced Magna Charta on him. Unsuccessful and very sick he died two months later.

NOTES

1. Notes on the dig are held in the Archaeological Section, Wilts County Council.
2. It was as archbishop that Dunstan was presiding over the *Witenagemot* (Assembly of the Wise Men) at Calne in the year 978 when according to the Anglo-Saxon Chronicles:

> All the chief Witan of the English nation fell from an upper chamber except the holy Archbishop Dunstan who alone supported himself on a beam. Some were grievously wounded and some did not excape with life.

Dunstan's friends proclaimed a miracle. His enemies (of whom he had many) claimed that he had arranged for the supporting timbers to be sawn almost through as a means of silencing the opposition.

2 THE MIDDLE AGES AND BEYOND

Peace and Prosperity

From the beginning Bradford had had what was needed to sustain life in comparative comfort; the means of good and durable shelter from the stone (jurassic oolite) never more than a few feet from the surface and food and clothing from the sheep grazing the surrounding chalk hills by day and folded by night to enrich the arable land. The long-drawn-out power struggle between barons and monarch which had begun in the reign of William the Conqueror's grandson Stephen was taking place elsewhere. Bradford was left undisturbed to grow and prosper, so much so that by the fourteenth century it was necessary to build a great barn as a storage place for the produce of Barton Farm and the tithe (one tenth) of the produce of all other land held in the manor of Bradford, payable in kind, to which the church was by law entitled.

In centuries to come some very large fortunes were made in the clothing industry and, as we shall see later, members of leading Bradford clothier families came to play their part on the national stage. But in the Middle Ages landowners were the rich and powerful ones.

Backwater though it still was in the late thirteenth century the town sometimes felt an eddy from the main stream. In 1295 King Edward I, at war with Scotland and Wales and under threat from continental Europe, found himself in dire financial straits. His remedy was to summon a parliament. He called representatives from every possible source of funds: earls, barons, archbishops and bishops, abbots and other church leaders, two knights from each shire and two representatives from each city and borough. It was the most representative assembly of its kind ever to be held in England up to then and for this reason is sometimes called the Model Parliament. Now designated as a borough (and a prosperous one at that) Bradford was obliged to comply and sent Thomas Dendans (or Dering) and William Wager; and the parliament having voted taxation, Bradford doubtless had to pay its whack. Thereafter the town was grateful to be left alone and, unlike neighbouring boroughs Calne, Chippenham, Devizes and Westbury, not called upon to be represented in parliament for the next 537 years.

The fourteenth century tithe-barn and (foreground left) the fifteenth century granary.

Tithe-barn interior, showing splendid cruck *(curved beam) trusses.*

The Chapel of St Mary the Virgin 'on the highest part of the town.'

Besides the tithe barn, and the charming stone bridge near by, one or two other buildings in the town still extant have their origins in the Middle Ages. Almost certainly one such is the little chapel or hermitage of St Mary the Virgin on Tory, though the earliest documentary date we have is 1540. In that year John Leland wrote in the course of his visit to the town: "Ther is a chappelle on the highest place of the town as I entered." When Thomas Bush Saunders rebuilt it in 1870 only part of the east wall was still standing.

At Priory House in Market Street the boundary wall bordering the road is medieval, all that remains of the substantial house built in the late 1400s by Thomas Rogers, Serjeant-at-Law. The present Priory House (see later) is the late Georgian extension originally built as a kitchen wing to the main house.

Number 11 Silver Street, the L-shaped shop known as "The Dairy", also has medieval origins. The east side of the L incorporates the roof and other remains of a building of the period 1350-1450 set gable-end to the road. The buildings in The Shambles on the post office side (but not the post office itself) are of the same era. The timber facades are a later, probably seventeenth century, modernisation.

The house called Barton Farm goes back in part at least to the medieval period and possibly to Saxon times. From the fact that in the early sixteenth century it was called the manor house it seems likely that it, or its predecessor on the site, was the manor house of the manor of Bradford given, as we have seen, by Aethelred to the Abbess of Shaftesbury in the year 1001. The building called the granary is fifteenth century, the tithe barn fourteenth century. Barton Farm covered a large acreage on both sides of the river Avon linked from at least the fourteenth century by Barton Bridge. Barton Bridge may also once have served a track which led from Salisbury Plain through Bath to Bristol and the sea.

Reminders of early Bradford linger. The house in Church Street called The Chantry, which itself goes back in part to the early sixteenth century, recalls the pre-Reformation practice of endowing a church or chapel with lands or other source of income for the maintenance of a

Barton Bridge linked Barton farmhouse and barn with farmlands north of the river from at least the fourteenth century. Bradford on Avon Rowing Club boats are kept near by.

priest or priests to sing or say mass daily for the soul of the donor or for the souls of persons named by him or her. The present building is almost certainly on the site of the priest's house of the chantry founded by Thomas Horton in 1524, one of three such known to have existed here. St Margaret's Street and St Margaret's Hill derive their names from St Margaret's Hospital, a medieval institution whose precise location is unknown. During his visit John Leland noted: "There is a litle streate over Bradford Bridge and at the ende of that is an hospitale of the Kinges of Englandes fundation."

This may have been the leper hospital dedicated to St Margaret, known to have been founded in 1235 and to have been under the patronage of Shaftesbury Abbey. That it had existed for some years before Leland we know from a deed of about 1459 and also from a will of 1490 which bequeathed six shillings and eightpence to poor inmates. A number of old buildings, among them the old poorhouse, in what was then called St Margaret's Street (but is now called Frome Road) were demolished when the railway cutting was made. If St Margaret's was indeed the leper hospital then a location away from the town centre, at that time on the north bank of the river, would be likely; so a reasonable guess would be that the old poorhouse had once been St Margaret's Hospital. Further along Frome Road are St Catherine's Almshouses, a foundation of great antiquity. In pre-Reformation days (notably 1535) twelve poor persons were receiving six shillings and eightpence yearly in return for offering prayers for the soul of the founder of Shaftesbury Abbey and this gives credence to oral tradition that in the Middle Ages it was a large establishment with its own chapel and chaplain.

Woolley Street derives its name from the chapel of St Olave, known to have existed in the late thirteenth century. Over the years the name evolved from *Seynt Olesstret* (early fifteenth century) to *Tooley Street* (eighteenth century) to its present style.

The Reformation

A king's marital and dynastic problems combined with the religious unrest which was disturbing all Christendom made for dangerous times. In Bradford the theological element of the equation gave rise to a burning at the stake; the political element brought to an end Shaftesbury Abbey's five centuries old manorial lordship.

Henry VIII, who up to 1535, notwithstanding his problems with the Vatican, saw himself as a good Catholic, was willing enough to allow a

St Catherine's Almshouses, Frome Road

burning at the stake for the benefit of the soul of the heretic concerned. Thus it was that Thomas Traynell, as we are told in a collection of traditional material published 1720-1731 by the Rev. J Cox and A Holly called *Magna Britannica et Hibernia antiqua et nova* or *A New Survey of Great Britain*, was burnt in Bradford in about 1532 around the same time and for the same reason as a fellow victim at Devizes; both were said to have denied transubstantiation, the doctrine that the bread and wine of the eucharist were literally the body and blood of Christ. This grisly event was doubtless held in the market place at the bottom of modern Market Street by the bridge foot.

But nationally events were moving rapidly. In 1533 Henry was excommunicated by Pope Clement VII because of his divorce from Catherine of Aragon. Within the next two decades Henry and his successor Edward VI had confiscated all church property, which in Bradford's case meant the Manor of Bradford and the chantries.

Of the two Bradford chantries extant in those days the one founded by Thomas Horton (a very rich clothier of whom more later) included a free school and on these grounds the townsfolk pleaded for its continuance. Their pleading partially succeeded. Although the chantry was dissolved, and its property sold to Richard Bellatt and to a nephew of Thomas Horton of the same name, money was made available for William Furbner, the former chantry priest, to continue teaching. (This happened elsewhere also and grammar schools called after Edward VI usually owe their existence to Edward's clemency.)

The other chantry, which seems to have been endowed by the Bird family of Marlborough, had been founded in 1524. William Bird, who was vicar of Bradford, held the appointment of chantry priest as well. He was also chaplain to Lord Hungerford of Heytesbury in respect of the castle at Farleigh Hungerford and this was to prove his undoing. In 1540 Hungerford went to the block on a charge of treason and Bird was likewise accused as his associate. Bird was convicted of using treasonable language against King Henry and was sacked from his living and forfeited the chantry house in which he had lived. Given the character of the man he was being tactless about – among other things he was reported to have called Henry a heretic – he was very lucky indeed not to finish up even more unpleasantly than his patron by being hanged, drawn and quartered, (the prescribed penalty for those not of the peerage). The chantry itself was dissolved about the same time.

3   EARNING A LIVING

I   "A TRULY NOBLE MANUFACTURE"

All the towne of Bradford stondith by cloth making.
John Leland (1506-1552)[1]

...the finest medley Spanish cloths, not in England only, but in the whole world, are made in this part. They told me at Bradford, That it was no extraordinary thing to have clothiers worth, from ten thousand to forty thousand pounds a man and many of the great families, who now pass for gentry in those counties, have been originally raised from, and built up by this truly noble manufacture.
Daniel Defoe (1660-1731)

From the fourteenth century on, promotion of the clothing industry was the paramount object of England's domestic and foreign policy. Under King Edward III import of cloth was prohibited, foreign clothworkers were invited to settle and teach their skills and clothiers were given special privileges. Later on (1678) a statute required bodies to be buried in cloth on pain of a substantial fine. Wars were waged to preserve markets overseas. If Old Caspar did not know why Blenheim was such a famous victory[2] Queen Anne's ministers certainly did. The industry shaped diplomacy and even served to change national drinking habits. Thus in 1703, the year before Blenheim, Anne's ambassador to Portugal, Bradford-born John Methuen (*c* 1650-1716), scion of the rich and powerful clothier family, negotiated the famous treaty by which

English cloth monopolised the Portuguese market in return for customs preferences for Portuguese wines over French ones. The cloth monopoly went long ago but the taste for port and madeira remains.

It was policy which the clothiers of Wiltshire and the Somerset border were well placed to exploit. Good quality wool was to hand. When power was needed fast-flowing rivers drove the mills. The opportunities were vast and they were ably exploited; by John Leland's day the character of Bradford as an important woollen town was already well established and in due course its clothiers would rank among the most powerful in the West Country. From this time on, the story of Bradford until the middle of the last century is largely the story of the clothing industry and its effects, direct and indirect, on town and people.

Fullers, Spinsters, Weavers, Scourers and Dyers

Right up to the eighteenth century the separate processes, from the sheep's back to man's, were, except fulling, hand work. Spinners (invariably female, hence the term spinster) and weavers nearly always worked at home with wheel (or distaff) and loom. So, for that matter, did their employers, the clothiers; which is why former weavers' cottages and clothiers' houses with remains of former workshops attached are so characteristic of Bradford today.

Other processes, scouring, fulling and dyeing called for abundant water and a degree of specialisation. The larger clothiers dyed on their own premises using their own dye-house, the smaller ones shared the facilities of a specialist dyer. The building now called St Margaret's Hall was originally (late eighteenth century) a specialist dyer's dye-house.

Scouring the wool was a stage before weaving, fulling the one immediately after it. Fulling was the process by which the cloth was shrunk and thickened (felted) by beating in water and fuller's earth with stocks (a kind of very large mallet). Water-power was harnessed for this in Bradford on Avon from very early on; one Adam le Folur was employing a powered mill here in 1249 - which makes him Bradford's earliest known industrialist. We happen to know about the Bradford mill because sadly, in that year, Adam's son John was found torn to pieces under the mill-wheel. (The verdict of the Court of Crown Pleas at the inquest was death by misadventure, nobody being suspected; but under the curious law of *deodand* (forfeiture to God) then in force the mill-wheel, as the instrument which had brought about the death, was declared forfeit, its value two shillings.[3]

The old dye-house, now St Margaret's Hall

Adam will also have needed running water for washing the wool and perhaps the woven cloth as well after its natural oil had all been removed by "scouring" – soaking in human urine. From the down-river side of Bradford town bridge may still be seen the remains of a little artificial island from which scoured wool used to be washed by hand in the stream as late as the latter part of the last century. Adam the Fuller probably had one just like it.

Bad Times and Good Ones
The industry had its ups and downs. The first half of the seventeenth century brought very hard times. An inept (and corrupt) government intervention in foreign trade in 1614 (the so-called Cockayne Experiment) sparked retaliation from the Dutch and in the trade war which followed our side got the worst of it. The market for Bradford's chief product, white broad-cloth, declined sharply while the demand for Dutch cloth grew. The slump lasted the better part of the next half century. Resentment and unrest found popular expression when in 1630 a commissioner of Charles I, Anthony Wither, came to investigate complaints about the quality of Bradford cloth; they threw him in the river. To make bad matters worse the town was afflicted by plague, once in 1609 and again in 1646.

It was not until after the Civil War (1642-1648)) that things began to
mend. The cloth that the Dutch were doing so well with was a high
quality product made from Spanish wool. There were technical
problems with spinning and weaving Spanish wool which the Dutch had
solved but the English had not. Then, in the 1650s, internationally-
minded Paul Methuen (died 1667) brought in a Dutch spinner to teach
his workers the special know-how. The plan seems to have succeeded.
In 1673/4 Trowbridge clothier William Brewer brought in 33 more and
three of them settled in Bradford; the house called Dutch Barton in
Church Street is a reminder of this, though strictly speaking Dutch
Barton, so Canon Jones tells us, was the yard of Abbey House (Thomas
Horton's house in Leland's day), a short way away.[4]

In sharp contrast to the state of affairs in the first half of the century
the second half was, thanks to the enterprise of such as Paul Methuen, a
time of prosperity and expansion. The town grew on both sides of the
river. There was new building on St Margaret's Hill and on the northern
slope where hitherto elderberries had been cultivated (and where
perhaps the vineyard recorded in Domesday Book had been located).
Newtown was created, then Middle Rank and building began at the east
end of Tory. Presbyterians, thanks to the Toleration Act of 1689 now,
with all other Protestants, free to worship as they wished, built
themselves the Grove Meeting House (now the Zion Baptist Chapel). In
1632 the town had been too impoverished even to keep the town bridge
in repair; now they not only repaired it but widened it by building
another one immediately alongside.

Scribbling Engines, Spinning Jennys and Gig Mills[5]

Bad times which afflicted master and man alike were bearable, even
though the former were better placed to cushion themselves against
them by careful investment, usually in land property, in the good times,
and in any case to transfer to the work force much of the misery of the
bad ones. Though there were disturbances in 1726 arising out of
allegations of cheating by the clothiers, they were of a different order
from what was to come later. The thrust of the century was invention
and innovation; and the machines which the masters had started to bring
in which enriched them and put most of their workers on the parish
provoked extreme resentment. Resort to violence was endemic. There
was a particularly ugly incident in 1791 when Joseph Phelps, who lived
on the job in what is now Westbury House, besieged by a threatening

Opposite: *Abbey Mill, built as a cloth mill in 1875, now used for rubber manufacture.*
Above: *Greenland Upper Mill, whose closure in 1905 marked the demise of Bradford's woollen industry.*

mob of workless, fired on them and killed three.

But the new scribbling engines (for preparing the wool for spinning), the spinning-jenny and spinning-mule, the gig-mill (for raising the nap) and the shearing frame, however much they might be resisted, could not be disinvented. They were available and they were profitable to use. They did not need a large, often recalcitrant, labour force but could be run with horse or water-power and later (when coal was readily available from the Somerset coal-fields via the Kennet and Avon Canal), by steam engine. And more and more they took work out of the cottage and on to the factory floor where it was more easily organised, controlled and supervised.

By the end of the century water power was being harnessed for most operations. In 1800 John Jones of Bradford erected at Staverton a grand water mill which a German visitor T A Nemnich described as "filled with every sort of newly invented machinery so that every kind of process except weaving can be done there."[6]

Thereafter low wages for those fortunate enough to be in work (and starvation for those who were not) created bitter resentment and sometimes outbreaks of violence. From Bradford in 1802 went a letter to parliament from "A Souldier Returned to his Wife and weeping Orphans" bitterly complaining about the machinery with the work-house "full of lurking boys" because of it; and that though setting fire to property was not right "Starvation forces Nature to do that which he would not."[7]

Decline and Fall

After Waterloo there was a steep fall in wages, rents and property prices throughout the country. As time went on things in Bradford went from bad to worse. In 1821 four weavers committed suicide in one day. In 1826 William Cobbett reported (in *Rural Rides*)that he had seen laid-off weavers and spinners from Bradford and elsewhere hand-digging a 12 acre field because wages had been forced so low that for the farmer it was "as cheap as ploughing and four times as good." At Heytesbury he was so moved by the plight of six men and two boys who had walked there from Bradford to get nuts that he went without his own supper and breakfast to give them a proper meal "for once in their lives." In 1815 there had been 30 manufacturers who produced in all 678 ends of broadcloth; in 1838 three manufacturers produced 144 ends. In 1840, of the 367 handlooms still in the town every second one was idle. It helped no-one when in the following year one of the local banks failed, partly from indifferent management and partly because of the slump.

By 1867 only two mills remained active, Greenland Upper Mill and one at the Bullpit. In 1875 a new building, Abbey Mill[8], was erected in Church Street but optimism proved misplaced. By 1902 it had closed and it remained empty until 1915 when it was taken over for rubber manufacture. In 1903 the last dye-house (now St Margaret's Hall) closed and in 1905 the last factory, Greenland Upper Mill, did likewise. The seven centuries old Bradford clothing industry was dead.

II BOUNCING BACK

In 1841, with all but a few looms idle and the failure of local bankers Hobhouse, Phillott and Lowder the outlook was bleak. But things were about to improve, though salvation came from an unexpected quarter.

It was in 1841 that an American called Charles Goodyear (1800-60) discovered how to process rubber in such a way as to make it less susceptible to the action of solvents and changes in temperature and improve its elasticity; in other words to retard "perishing" and render it more versatile. Among Goodyear's acquaintances was an Englishman, a New York broker called Stephen Moulton (1794-1880). Failing to interest American manufacturers, Goodyear asked Moulton to approach the Macintosh company or some other British manufacturer. Charles Macintosh (1766-1843) was a Glasgow chemical manufacturer who had, since 1824, been treating fabric with rubber solution to make waterproof garments ("macintoshes").

Examining the samples of Goodyear's product which Moulton took to England with him in 1842 Thomas Hancock (1786-1865), Macintosh's partner, also a chemist, concluded that if Goodyear could do it he could too; and he set to work and did. He and Macintosh obtained British patents in 1843, forestalling Goodyear here. At the suggestion of Hancock's friend Brockedon they called the process vulcanization.

Convinced that rubber spelt profitable business, Stephen Moulton returned to England to set up in it himself. Bradford's deserted woollen mills on the banks of the Avon with its clean running water offered him just what he needed. In 1848 he bought Kingston House together with the adjacent Kingston Mill, both semi-derelict, and some other smaller deserted mills near by. Steam-engines and water-wheels were already installed and in working order and Moulton was to use both for many

Stephen Moulton (1794-1880) founding father of Bradford's rubber industry.

years until they were superseded by electricity, itself at first generated on the spot by steam engine and turbine. About this time a friend of Moulton's, Captain Septimus Palairet, who had recently married an American heiress and retired from the army, came to live at Woolley Grange (see later). Palairet also foresaw a bright future for rubber and put up £5,000 to help get things going.

The venture was timely and went well from the start. The new vulcanization technology was put to good and profitable effect to manufacture waterproof clothing for our troops in the Crimea; and new railways throughout the world proved a splendid outlet for hoses for braking and heating and the rubber springs for rolling stock which George Spencer and Co. had patented in 1852 and which Moulton manufactured under licence from him.

George Spencer, Moulton Ltd.

In 1891 George Spencer and the Moulton brothers Horatio and John, Stephen's sons, floated George Spencer, Moulton Ltd. and in due course took over more abandoned cloth factories, including, in 1915, the Church Street and Abbey Mills. By this time waterproof clothing manufacture was long over but the company continued to be world-renowned for design, development and manufacture of products for railways. As time went on automobile and aircraft products were added to the range; also tennis balls. In 1919 a new factory was erected on the site of the Lamb Inn which had stood in the old market place at the northern end of the town bridge.

Avon Industrial Polymers

In 1956 George Spencer, Moulton and Co. became part of the much larger Avon Rubber Company, with its many subsidiary companies in Britain and overseas, and was renamed Avon Industrial Polymers. At Bradford the Moulton tradition of equipment for railway rolling stock has continued, but nowadays it is buffers, drawgear and suspension components for high-speed *125 Intercity* trains. It continues, too, its automobile industry links, manufacturing windscreen wipers, wind-screen seals and engine mountings.

Non-traditional, in fact bang up-to-date and original is a product used successfully on offshore oil platforms to overcome the problem of encrustation by barnacles and seaweed. This consists of rubber matting impregnated with grains of cupro-nickel which is wrapped around the parts likely to be affected to make an ecologically acceptable electrolytic deterrent. Last, but certainly not least, is the production of aerosol gaskets and cup seals used in virtually every aerosol manufactured world-wide; seven billion of these leave Bradford every year. There are some 500 employees at the Bradford works.

III INDUSTRIES OLD AND NEW

Stone Quarrying
Quarrying for the Cotswold Limestone (jurassic oolite) so readily available is undoubtedly Bradford's oldest continuing industrial activity. The stone produced today (at Westwood) is used mainly for repair and restoration work. Cotswold Limestone is easily sawn and worked but extremely durable; the Saxon church, the town's oldest building, will have been built of stone quarried almost on the spot.

The stone tiles traditionally used for roofing are of forest marble, a much harder stone. Forest marble forms the bedrock at Budbury. The 1841 tithe map (item 1806) shows a tile quarry near Midford.

Bradford stands on the very edge of the belt of Great and Inferior Oolite which runs in a winding strip from Dorset to Yorkshire; to the east of the town is Cornbrash and Oxford Clay.

Malting and Brewing
Beer has been the Englishman's tipple from time out of mind. Right up to the middle of the last century Bradford's inns and ale-houses brewed their own beer and sometimes made their own malt as well. We know, for example, that Richard Pearce, the eighteenth century Bradford Methodist who kept the Maidenhead Inn (now the Town Club) in Market Street had his own malthouse behind the pub. But malting was a specialist craft, needing space under cover for sprouting the grain and a kiln for processing it and most publicans were content to leave it to the professionals.

In the heyday of the clothing industry small malthouses proliferated. serving the numerous public houses. In 1841, though the industry was in serious decline, there were still 19 public houses and four malthouses. The malthouse which operated in Frome Road (1841 tithe map item 789) which was then owned by George and Thomas Spencer is commemorated in the name of the flats there, The Maltings. Of the other specialist malthouses shown on the map, one (item 550) was run by William Coles, the ironfounder (see below) at his premises off Trowbridge Road, another (item 580) owned by Richard and John Bethel and run by Richard Blackmore was on the south-west side of Trowbridge Road (Poulton) and the fourth was in Church Street (item 180 – *house and malthouse)* adjacent to Trinity Church Hall.

In 1842, bad times notwithstanding, Alexander Wilkins, a member of the family who ran the nearby Seven Stars Inn (now a private house) where hitherto they had malted and brewed on a small scale for their own pub, erected in Newtown the fortress-like Seven Stars Maltings and Brewery. This operated up to the First World War. Now Long's builders yard, it stands dilapidated but still impressive, with the seven metal stars of its trade name still fixed firmly in the stone boundary wall.

Small-Scale Engineering
Until the early 1800s such engineering skills as were needed by the farm or the mill were to be found in the blacksmith's forge or at the carpenter's bench. But times were changing. By 1822 John and Job Wastfield were established as makers of water-wheels and shearing frames and William Coles was running a foundry behind his house in Trowbridge Road; it stood near where Blackwell's now is. (He also ran a malthouse there, see above). As time went on the demand for agricultural machinery grew and after about 1850 when George Milsom took over Coles's iron foundry, he added brass founding and agricultural engineering. About the same time his brother Charles, millwright and engineer, had works "near the bridge".

The Moulton rubber development created even more demand for local engineering enterprise. S J Brierley (Wilts) Ltd.,"mechanical engineers, millwrights and merchants" operated at 87 Trowbridge Road mainly for the rubber works and we find Berkley Uncles, Milsom's former apprentice, who took over from him in 1899, doing likewise. Uncles manufactured mouldings and castings to order; drain and manhole covers bearing the name are still in use in the town. Other foundries were run by H Crisp (Avonside Iron Foundry) and H Martin who among other things cast grave markers; specimens of this work may be seen in the Holt Road cemetery.

Moulton Developments Ltd.
A small but successful engineering business is carried on by this company. It manufactures the latest version of the small-wheel Moulton bicycle introduced in 1962 by Alex Moulton (great-grandson of Stephen Moulton, founder of the Bradford rubber industry) which in 1964 received the Design Centre Award. Production of that particular model was taken over by the Raleigh Company in 1967 and discontinued in 1974. The current model is the very Rolls Royce of small-wheel pedal bicycles, hand-crafted for excellence and possessing the unusual characteristic that the frame can be dismantled for easy stowage in a matter of seconds. Annual output is some 1000 machines, created in a small workshop in the grounds of the Hall. Some dozen workers are employed.

M Y Sports and Games Ltd. Greenland Mills
This is a branch of a London company, M Y Sports and Games Ltd., itself a subsidiary of M Y Dart plc, manufacturers and distributors of sports equipment. At Bradford they make tennis balls, ping-pong balls, dart-flights and referees' whistles. The Bradford operation was started some 40 years ago as the Rex Rubber Company. There are 73 employees.

Trio Plastic Products Ltd.
This company was established in 1975 for the manufacture of glassfibre reinforced plastic products to the firm's own design (for example modular insulated cabins, tanks and glassfibre planters) or to customers' specific requirements (for example automobile body panels, machine guards and building cladding panels). There are about sixteen employees.

W Darlington and Sons Ltd.
Bradford's largest stone quarries were underground. Such spent underground quarries, with their stable humidity and even temperatures (average natural temperature 52 to 54 degrees Fahrenheit boosted with an oil-fired boiler to 62 to 63 degrees Fahrenheit), are ideal for growing mushrooms. The Bradford branch of mushroom-growers W Darlington and Sons Ltd, one of the largest companies in the business, is among their most extensive, with 14 acres underground and 56,000 square feet of bed area in crop all the time.

Mushroom-growing in Bradford goes back to the 1870s when a Mr Robinson grew mushrooms in Bethell Quarry for making into ketchup. In 1921 Agaric Ltd. set up here; they had been in the business since 1914, first in Surrey, then from 1919 at Corsham. France was the first country to adopt underground cultivation and from the beginning Agaric used French methods; in Bradford they employed French experts. (One of these was Monsieur C Baumann; he settled in the town and descendents of his still live here.) Agaric became W Darlington and Sons Ltd, a member of the H J Heinz group of companies, in 1970. There are some 90 employees at the Bradford farm.

Weir Electrical Instrument Company Ltd.

The Weir Electrical Instrument Company, located at Greenland Mills, was formed in 1937 to manufacture electrical indicating instruments and associated equipment for educational and industrial use. This continues, but since the 1950s another important product has been the *Buchholz Relay* which the company supplies to the Central Electricity Generating Board and the electricity generating industry generally for the protection of their large supply transformers. The market is world-wide.

Since 1985 the company has been run as a family business with E R Irving, a former technical and works manager, as managing director. The company employs 33 persons.

William Dotesio (Printers) Ltd. Greenland Mills

This company has its origins in the printing and stationery business at 28 Silver Street which William Charles Dotesio started in the 1890s. After service in the First World War brothers William Henry (1901-1971) and Eric Ben (died 1976) joined their father in the business and in due course took charge. In 1931 they formed William Dotesio (Printers) Ltd. The firm moved to larger premises at 17 Silver Street (now Moxham's Antiques) and continued there until 1934. In that year they moved to the present location at Greenland Mills.

In 1979 the company was taken over by Top Ten Promotions Ltd. of Bristol but continues to trade under its old name. The Bradford company specialises in loose-leaf, journal and book printing and binding, its principal outlets being major publishing houses throughout the United Kingdom. There are 62 employees at the Bradford works.

BRADFORD ON AVON PAST AND PRESENT

Snuff, Twine and even a Windmill

Tobacco was widely grown in Wiltshire in the seventeenth century. At Devizes the firm of Anstie Ltd. was in the snuff and tobacco business until 1960. In the eighteenth century years of depression a Bradford cloth mill went over to producing snuff but the venture was shortlived. It hardly seems enough to justify the epithet "snuffy" sometimes applied to Bradfordians!

At one time twine was made in Newtown. In the 1970s Mr F King, who had lived in Bradford for 82 years, recalled that when he was at the primary school (which stood where the Rope Walk flats now stand) he would see men at work in what he called the twine yards. Making twine in those days was clearly highly labour-intensive; Mr King described the men "walking backwards with the hemp all round their waist" while a wheel revolved to spin the twine.

Another short-lived enterprise was Thomas Smart's tower windmill, which, in the early 1800s, he erected just off Mason's Lane on land bought not long before from Thomas Edwards the Elder. Smart was a baker who thought to turn his hand to milling and in 1808 was advertising for help. The scheme was clearly a mistake. The next we hear of the building is that it has become a private house and that Thomas Smart is living in it. The mill is today a guest-house.

Thomas Smart's tower windmill, now called The Round House.

40

IV CANAL AND RAILWAY

A canal to link the Kennet Navigation at Newbury with the Avon Navigation at Bath to provide a waterway between Bristol and London was authorised by Parliament in 1794. The work was begun in October that year (starting, incidentally, at Bradford) and was complete by 1810.

Bradford was an important port of call and had two wharves, one above the lock and one below it. Trade was brisk. Barges carried goods of every description to and from Bath, Bristol and London and passenger vessels travelled daily between those destinations; Murhill Quarry had its own quarry wharf. Coal from the Somerset coal fields, brought by way of the Somerset Coal Canal which joined the Kennet and Avon at Limpley Stoke, fed the nearby gasworks when gaslighting was brought to the town in the 1830s.

But the canal's era of prosperity was soon over. With the coming of the Great Western Railway in mid-century the canal company were out-rivalled and in 1852 they found themselves obliged to sell to the railway company. The canal nevertheless remained navigable and continued in use until the 1950s. Thereafter it was deserted and rapidly became overgrown along much of its length. Since then, however, the Kennet and Avon Canal Trust, in cooperation with the British Waterways Board, has gradually been restoring it and it is likely to be open along the whole length in the not too distant future. From Bradford it is already navigable to Bath to the west and Lower Foxhangers to the east. At Bradford plans have been made for a marina for 100 leisure craft.

By 1848 the Wilts, Somerset and Weymouth Railway Company, which had been formed in 1844 to create a rail link between Weymouth and Bathampton, had built railway stations at Bradford and Trowbridge. In the same year a line between Chippenham and Trowbridge was opened. But to the dismay of Bradfordians, for the next nine years their station stood in the middle of a field unconnected to anything. Money had run out and investors had become chary. Among other things the length to Bathampton had proved more expensive than had been envisaged. The construction of seven viaducts and more especially two aqueducts, one to carry the Kennet and Avon canal over the line at Avoncliff and the other to do the same at Limpley Stoke had posed engineering problems. At Avoncliff, burrowing under the canal put it out of commission for a while and there were major problems with the creation of the Dundas aqueduct at Limpley Stoke – "a tedious and

Above: *Bradford Wharf on the Kennet and Avon Canal, for many years out of use, now once again in business, though only for pleasure. With the coming of the Great Western Railway the canal, outmoded, went into decline.*

Below: *Bradford on Avon Railway Station, built in 1848 but not brought in to use until 1857.*

rather difficult operation" Brunel called it. In 1850 the W S W R company went into liquidation and its assets were taken over by the Great Western Railway.

In 1857, at long last, the line through Bradford was finished and passed inspection; and on the 2nd February, by way of celebration, a free special left Bradford station for Weymouth.

NOTES

1. John Leland (c 1506-1552), chaplain to Henry VIII and his Library Keeper, was appointed King's Antiquary in 1533 and commissioned to search ecclesiastical establishments throughout the country for records and manuscripts. Between 1536 and 1542 he toured the whole of England. Besides his main purpose he made notes on the places he visited. In 1540 he visited Bradford and much of what we know about what the town was like then we owe to these notes.

Leland intended his researches to be the basis of a great work on "The History and Antiquities of the Nation" but did not live to accomplish it. He lost his reason in 1550 and died two years later. *Leland's Itinerary* was published in 9 volumes in 1710 and *Collectanea* in six volumes in 1715.

2. I refer to John Southey's ironic lines:
   " And everybody praised the Duke,
   Who this great fight did win."
   "But what good came of it at last?"
   Quoth little Peterkin.
   "Why that I cannot tell" said he
   "But 'twas a famous victory."
The Battle of Blenheim in 1704 took place in the course of the War of the Spanish Succession (1702-13). At Blenheim, on the River Danube in Germany, the English army under the Duke of Marlborough destroyed the French one. As a result of this and other setbacks King Louis XIV of France was rendered powerless to close Spain – and therefore South America and the Mediterranean – to English cloth. Gibraltar was seized at the same time and for the same reason.

3. A similar accident happened at Avoncliff in the same year but in this instance the owner was a miller, William by name. The victim was a youth called David.

4. Article in *Wiltshire Archaeological Magazine* Vol. XX page 306.

5. The gig mill replaced "teasing" (raising the nap) by hand. Both methods used the head of the teasel *(dipsacus fullonum)* fixed in a frame called a "handle". The cloth was damped for teasing and handles needed to be dried after use. "Handle-houses" were used for this. At Bearfield there is a cottage called the Round House (12 Bearfield Buildings) which is believed to have been erected originally, in the late eighteenth or early nineteenth century, as a handle-house.

6. Quoted by K G Ponting in *Wool and Water*. The building, minus four of its original six storeys, but still impressive, belongs now to the Nestle Co.

7. E P Thompson: *The Making of the Working Class* quoting Hammond: *The Skilled Labourer*.

8. This excellent building was designed by a leading London architect, Richard Gane. In 1971 it was restored by Avon Industrial Polymers Ltd.

4   CHURCHES, CHAPELS AND MEETING HOUSES

I   PARISH CHURCHES

The Saxon Church
With the coming of the Normans, and the building by them near by of a grander church, the one built by the Saxons will have fallen gradually into disuse. We hear of it again in 1614 when Gifford Yerbury is stated to have held a "chappell" and other property by copyhold from the lord of the manor. What the old Saxon church was used for during the next 100 years we do not know but in 1715 we find it being called variously the "skull-house" and "the bone-house", which suggests that it had become, in part at least, an ossuary. Then in about 1710 it was converted, probably by the rector of the day, into a free school for boys of Bradford parish. We know from the Charity Commissioners' report of 1834 that the premises then comprised "an underground cellar, two rooms and garret above stairs, one room and a small pantry below, a large school room, kitchen underneath, a recess adjoining, commonly called the bone-house, and a small place attached to the school-house for the convenience of the boys." The report commented that the whole building was in a very dilapidated state.

In about 1856 repair work happened to uncover carvings in stone of two angels over what we now know was the original chancel arch. Thus alerted, the archaeologically-minded vicar of Holy Trinity, Canon W H R Jones, discovered, submerged in the accretions of the centuries, the outlines of the nave and chancel of a small church. A few years later J T Irvine, an architect well known for his distinguished work on Bath

Abbey and other important buildings also began to take an interest in it. It was, however, still in part the charity school in the hands of trustees and in part a separate cottage in private hands, so it was not yet possible to consider restoration. But from 1869 Irvine did a number of sketches which, together with his notes, form an excellent record of the building as it was before restoration and at the various stages in its rehabilitation. (These notes and drawings are in Bath reference library.) Then one day in 1871, Canon Jones, browsing in the Bodleian library at Oxford, came upon a recently-published book containing the text of the *Gesta Pontificum* of William of Malmesbury. The following passage caught his eye:

> Et est ad hunc diem eo loco ecclesiola quam ad nomen beatissima Laurentii fecisse predicatur Aldhelmus.

> At that place [*viz* Bradford] there is to this day a little church which Aldhelm is said to have built to the name of the most blessed Laurence.

The words had been written in about the year 1125. Here was clear confirmation of the church's considerable antiquity and evidence (admittedly hearsay) that it was even older than had hitherto been supposed, though Jones, in a letter to Irvine, was cautious enough to comment only that the passage carried back the little church "to the beginning of the twelfth century at all events". He also reported that he had succeeded in purchasing the chancel (hitherto occupied as a cottage) and a plot of ground all round sufficient to isolate it within boundary walls.

Thereafter there was steady progress. A trust was formed (the first trustees were, besides Jones, Lord Nelson, Sir John Awdry, Sir Charles Hobhouse, J H Parker and the Rev. E L Barnwell) and fund-raising begun. In June 1874 the trustees were in full possession of the entire building, having exchanged it for Old Church House (now called Trinity Church Hall), a few yards down the street, to which the school was then transferred. Irvine was appointed architect for the restoration; but Canon Jones, in his enthusiasm to press on with the work, brought in a local architect also. Work was done of which Irvine disapproved as out of keeping. In 1881 he resigned specifically over the trustees' instructions that the master's house should be demolished and replaced with buttresses.

The Saxon Church of St Laurence

Above: *Saxon stone carvings on the chancel arch.*

Below: *Blind arcading on the east wall. The pilasters are characteristic of late Saxon work.*

47

The Church of the Holy Trinity

If the monastery which the Danes destroyed in about 1015 was indeed built by Aldhelm when he became abbot of Malmesbury in the year 675; and if, as seems possible, the original Saxon Church building was built alongside about the same time, then the area where the parish church of the Holy Trinity stands has been hallowed by Christian worship for over 1,300 years.

Holy Trinity is usually dated back to about 1150 on the basis that the little church that William of Malmesbury was writing about in 1125 was the only one in the parish. But we know that William the Conqueror was a dedicated ecclesiastical reformer and that by the time of his death in 1087 all the Saxon bishops had been replaced by Norman ones and Saxon church buildings were being replaced or rebuilt in the Romanesque (or Norman) style. The very fact that a Saxon church was there to be snubbed argues for an earlier date; and William of Malmesbury does call the Saxon church by the diminutive *ecclesiola* - as if it were not the principal one. So Holy Trinity *could* be older than mid-twelfth century.

What we see today from the outside is not so very different from what a twelfth century Bradfordian would have seen. The Normans built a nave, a chancel and a tower. The chancel was lengthened about a century later. The tower is different; the present one was probably erected in the fifteenth century. The building is wider; in about the fifteenth century the north wall was pierced and arched and the nave extended to create what is now an aisle but which in pre-Reformation days will have formed the Hall, Bird and Horton chantry chapels mentioned earlier. On the south side is an extension, now used as the sacristy but built as a chapel in about the sixteenth century, possibly by a member of the Hall family. Our twelfth century Bradfordian would recognise the window over the south door and the round-headed windows of the chancel, but none of the others.

Over the years the interior of the building has suffered at the hands of reformers and also at the hands of unsympathetic or over-enthusiastic restorers. Preserved at the west end of the nave is all that remains of the pre-Reformation painted rood screen, showing two figures with a manuscript with verses from the opening chapter of St John's gospel; the rest of the screen will have been torn down at the time of the Reformation.

Immediately below is all that remains of a full-size thirteenth or fourteenth century stone female effigy, discovered in the 1860s; it was

Hallowed by Christian worship for over 1,300 years? Here, where Bishop Aldhelm's monastery probably once stood, stand side by side the Saxon and Norman churches and the chantry house (seen to the right of the church tower). On the skyline is the chapel of St Mary, Tory.

found, charming wimpled[1] face down, having been used to repair paving. Because effigies of females of that date are rare it has been conjectured that the lady commemorated was a member of the rich and powerful Hall family, perhaps Agnes, wife of Reginald de Aula who died in 1250.

Near by is a facsimile of the so-called Bishop's Bible[2] of 1572. The original volume, now safely in the Wiltshire Record Office, was discovered for sale in a Bradford second-hand furniture shop.

Interesting features in the north aisle are the carved stone ornamentation in the north wall, most probably the reredos to the altar of one of the chantry chapels, and the 18 foot long squint (perhaps the longest in England), pierced through the original Norman north wall. On the east wall and to the left of the squint is a brass commemorating Thomas Horton (died 1530), the rich Bradford clothier and property-owner, and his wife Mary, prepared in their lifetimes (dates of deaths left to be inserted later but the job never done) with Thomas's merchant's mark – the mark he attached to his bales of cloth – displayed and Thomas clearly as proud of it as any nobleman of his coat of arms. Nearby in the north wall is the stained glass window commemorating Canon W H Jones, vicar, celebrated Bradford historian and antiquary and discoverer, as we have seen, of the long-lost Saxon Church; and next to it, interestingly, one to his contemporary, Joseph Rawling, Methodist minister at Lady Huntingdon's chapel. Rawling died in 1866 and Jones in 1885 so the window evidently had the good canon's approval.

A window on the south wall has stained glass of Flemish origin consisting of a number of roundels depicting scenes from the life of Jesus; this was the gift of John Ferret (1702-70).

Holy Trinity has a splendid peal of eight bells (two of them cast in 1615) a clock without a dial (but which strikes the quarters as well as the hour) and a carillon. Before 1913 there was a "set of chimes" which performed the tunes of *Hanover* and *The Sicilian Mariners' Hymn* every three hours. In 1913 a carillon by Gillett and Johnson of Croydon was installed which plays the tunes of four hymns, *Holy, Holy, Holy; Jerusalem my Happy Home; God Moves in a Mysterious Way;* and *The Sicilian Mariners' Hymn.*

Christ Church

The juxtaposition of great riches and dire poverty was characteristic of Victorian England. By the middle of the century much of Bradford was badly run down; towards the end of it an official report described the area near the parish church where Trinity Church Hall (then the Free Grammar School) stands as being "in a bad part of the town", and just across the river from it the British School was closed by the authorities because of its unsavoury surroundings. But high on the hill on the northern outskirts things were very different. Berryfield House (now the hospital) was built in about 1840 and around the same time Frankleigh House (now the Old Ride Preparatory School) was refurbished on the grand scale. A few years later Captain Palairet re-modelled Woolley Grange. Money in some pockets was plentiful and what better use for it than to build a brand-new church?

Christ Church was, accordingly, commissioned in 1839 and consecrated two years later. It was designed by G P Manners of Bath and erected by Jones Brothers of Bradford. It cost £3,862, raised by public subscription.

A contemporary painting of the interior shows plain glass windows, plain walls and stone-flagged floor. This "style of rigid simplicity", as Canon Jones called it, was far *too* simple for the taste of Victorian England, and in 1875 the new vicar, Richard Umfraville Lambert (1829-1905), set about remedying matters. The famous church architect Sir Gilbert Scott was engaged and produced the design for the building much as we see it today, chancel added beyond the present communion rail, altar raised, choir stalls created, a new organ installed, gallery removed, all the pews changed for new ones, walls decorated, stained glass introduced and gas-lighting fitted on wrought-iron chandeliers. Almost Scott's last work, Jones commented in the Wiltshire Archaeological Magazine in August 1881, that it was now "well worth a visit."

There were further changes after the First World War. The Lady Chapel was added by the Moulton family as a memorial to Eric Moulton, killed in action in France in 1916; and in 1923 the peal of eight bells was given by Brigadier General Palmer of Berryfield House (now Bradford on Avon hospital, see later).

The first incumbent was perpetual curate John Hopkins Bradney (died 1861) who lived at Leigh House (see later) which he bought in 1840 presumably in anticipation of his appointment the following year.

The parsonage, at 3 Mason's Lane, was acquired by the Ecclesiastical Commissioners in 1844 and was occupied by the Reverend J C Earle who succeeded Bradney as vicar. It had been built as a private house some time after 1819 by James Budgett[3].

The old town hall, now the Roman Catholic Church of St Thomas More.

CHURCHES, CHAPELS AND MEETING HOUSES

The Roman Catholic Church of St Thomas More

In 1955, after the lapse of centuries, a Roman Catholic parish once again came into being to serve Bradford, Holt, Monkton Farleigh, Westwood, Winsley, and Wraxall. The church building is the one-time town hall in Market Street, which assumed its latest role on June 25, 1955, when Dr Joseph Rudderham, Bishop of Clifton gave the inaugural blessing.

The building was exactly 100 years old. In its day it had housed Bradford Urban District Council, a masonic lodge and a cinema. It was designed by Thomas Fuller (1822 – 1898) of Bath[4] and erected by James Long on behalf of a private company for leasing to Bradford Urban District Council. It remained the council offices until 1910, when the owners put it up for sale. The council having refused to buy, it then became the town's first cinema.

II NONCONFORMITY AND DISSENT

Il y a en Angleterre soixante sectes religieuses différentes, et une seule sauce.

In England they have sixty different religious sects but only one sauce.

(Attributed to Voltaire)

If Queen Elizabeth could spurn the Vatican, her subjects could, at least, disagree with the Church of England. Or so they seemed to think. The Elizabethan establishment would doubtless have preferred all to submit themselves to the established church, and indeed, it was unlawful not to attend. After Elizabeth's death in 1603 English Protestantism seemed at risk, her Stuart successors being Roman Catholics at heart. But towards the century's end the "Glorious Revolution" (1688) which unseated Rome-inclined James II finally brought to rest the Catholic-Protestant see-saw which Henry VIII had set in motion a century and a half before. By this time Protestant dissenting sects abounded and one of the first actions of the new monarchy of William and Mary was to acknowledge their right to worship in their own way provided their place of worship was formally registered with the local magistrates.

We know from the records of these registrations[5] that in Bradford there have been Baptists, Congregationalists, Independents, Methodists, Presbyterians, Quakers and Unitarians. Today we have the Old Baptist Chapel, the Bearfield Congregational Church, the Quakers (Religious Society of Friends), the United Church and the Zion Baptist Chapel, all with ancestry rooted in the seventeenth century.

The Old Baptist Chapel

The Baptists had secured a strong foothold in England, first in London in 1612, then in the country at large. The Old Baptist Chapel in St Margaret's Street derives its origins from the first-comers from before 1672; in that year they registered John Broome's barn as their place of worship. Seventeen years later they built a chapel to hold 300 on land off St Margaret's Street belonging to Zachariah Shrapnel. This was rebuilt on the same site in 1797. Though, like other religious bodies everywhere, the Bradford church has suffered its schisms,the chief of which occurred in 1842, when part of the congregation left to join the Independents at Zion Chapel (see below), the Chapel in St Margaret's Street, from its inauguration up to today, has never lacked a congregation.

The Grove Meeting House

Now called Zion Baptist Chapel, the Grove Meeting House which stands at the eastern end of Middle Rank was erected in 1698 by Presbyterians. Presbyterianism, which had been established in England under Cromwell, was strong in this country until about the middle of the eighteenth century. Thereafter it declined; members seceded in groups or just drifted away, some to become Baptists, others Independents, others Unitarians.

Before they built the Grove Meeting House Bradford Presbyterians had been worshipping from at least 1672 at the house of John Holton; and twenty years later at Francis Yerbury's house or in his barn, both of which places were registered[6].

By 1739 the Grove Meeting House congregation was leaning heavily towards Unitarianism. The minister, Dr Joshua Read, found this not to his liking and with his supporters left (see later). His successor was Dr Roger Flexman (1708-95)[7] from Chard, Presbyterian and Calvinist. In Bradford he married a member of his congregation, Catharine, daughter of clothier John Yerbury (1678-1728).

In January 1793 the Grove Meeting House congregation adopted the Unitarian liturgy, though they still called themselves Presbyterians.

54

The Grove Meeting House (now Zion Baptist Church) built in 1698, the oldest non-conformist place of worship in the town.

Among the leaders were men of good standing in the town, including rich clothiers John William Yerbury and his brother-in-law John Moggridge. But by 1815 the congregation had dwindled to almost nothing and shortly afterwards the building was being used by the Independents who had separated from Morgan Hill (see below). From 1823 Zion Chapel, which they had built on the Conigre across the way, was their place of worship.

In 1842 they were joined by a group who had seceded from the Baptists in St Margaret's Street (see above).Thereafter they called themselves Particular Baptists or Zion Chapel Baptists.

The Grove Meeting House remained in Presbyterian ownership but was used by them only occasionally. In 1876, following Charity Commission investigations, it was vested in the Official Trustee of

Charity Lands. From about this time the Zion Baptists rented it as an annex, then in 1939 they closed Zion Chapel and made Grove Meeting House their main place of worship. Zion Baptist Chapel continues at the Grove Meeting House, which not only makes it the oldest nonconformist place of worship in the town but also the only one to be used continuously as such since its erection nearly three centuries ago.

Zion Chapel was demolished in the wave of destruction which afflicted the town in the 1960s.

The United Church, St Margaret's Hill

The Presbyterians who under Dr Joshua Read seceded from the Grove in January 1739 built a new chapel on Morgan Hill (now St Margaret's Hill) on land given by Sarah Grant (died 1741) of Bradford. Walter Grant of Monkton Farleigh, Sarah's brother, John Pitman of Bradford and Joshua Read himself each gave £100. The chapel opened in 1741 and was registered as Independent.

The stone tablet on the front of the building records that it was built as an Independent Meeting in 1740 and enlarged in 1798 and 1835.

In 1815 disagreement with the trustees about their powers in relation to the pastor led to a split and the dissidents left and took over the Grove, as stated above. Attempts at reconciliation failed, but were not totally fruitless; the trustees relinquished the powers which had started the row. Today the church is the forward-looking and ecumenically-minded United Church, comprising the United Reformed and Methodist Churches, with antecedents including Congregational and English Presbyterian churches.

Bearfield Congregational Church

This congregation maintains its long tradition of independence.

The building was erected in 1787 as Bethel Chapel. It was registered as Independent, the property of Caleb Hodges "and others". The liturgy was Anglican. After only a few years it closed. The history of the present persuasion begins with its purchase by the Reverend Thomas Watkins of Bath. Watkins died in 1802 and left the chapel to his widow, who in 1806 married Joseph Rawling, a schoolmaster and preacher from Ide in Devon. Rawling was in pastoral charge till his death in 1816. Not long after this the chapel was taken over by Lady Huntingdon's Connexion (originally upper-crust Methodist-become-Calvinist[8] and from 1790 separated from Wesleyan Methodism). Its memory lingers in Bradford in the name of the street where it was located, but its impact here was slight, its congregation not at all what Lady Huntingdon had in mind.

When Joseph Rawling (1792-1866) grandson of the Joseph Rawling who had been minister up to 1816 agreed in 1847 to take charge (without stipend) he did so partly because he was sorry for the far from well-off members, seven in all, in their dilapidated chapel, and partly in his grandfather's memory. He thought of it as deserting Methodism and regretted leaving the chapel on Coppice Hill of which he had been steward since it opened in 1818. But as things turned out he was able to preserve links and later on we find him preaching at Coppice Hill and at Zion Chapel, too, on occasion.

Rawling made the chapel the love of his life. In 1849 overdue repairs were carried out and shortly afterwards he installed an organ. The congregation was never large, but it did survive. Fourteen years after his death it became Congregationalist, a natural step given its Calvinist antecedents, though for many years it was still known as Lady Huntingdon's Chapel.

Providence Baptist Chapel, Bearfield

This chapel was opened in 1858. Its congregation was never large and it has now ceased to be a place of worship. The present intention is to convert the building to residential accommodation.

Methodism

On Tuesday 17 July 1739 John Wesley rode into Bradford from Bath for the first of many visits. He had looked forward to fruitful co-operation with Joshua Read, the Presbyterian minister whom he had met in Bath, and in his journal he records his disappointment at being rebuffed by him. What he will not have known at the time was that, as we have seen, Read had recently left the Grove in a huff and must have been under stress. Read was no doubt fearful of the effect Wesley might have on his already diminished flock, particularly since, as he told Wesley, he had heard that he had been regarded at Oxford as a little crack-brained. Moreover, he had, for the time being, no church premises of his own, only John Pitman's house as a place of worship.

Wesley was almost as disappointed with the vicar, John Rogers, who was not willing to make his church available on a week-day, though he declared himself glad of assistance on a Sunday. (Wesley was, of course, an ordained priest of the Anglican communion).

Paradoxically Wesley had better luck with the Quakers. After preaching at Bearfield to an audience of about 1,000 he called on Constant Bailward[9], Quaker minister, widow of a rich Quaker clothier, and so began what was to become a lifelong association with the Bailward family.

Wesley was greatly attracted to Bradford and seems to have been exceptionally well received. He preached at Bearfield some half dozen times in the year of his first visit to audiences of (he claimed) up to 10,000. Over the next 50 years he visited the town on 26 occasions.

The first registration of a Methodist place of worship in Wiltshire was at Bradford, in 1756. The licence describes it as "lately erected adjoining the dwellinghouse of John Silby" and the applicants were "John Silby and others". It had been built by Richard Pearce landlord of the Maidenhead Inn in Pippet Street (now Market Street), behind his pub, where a malthouse had been. Pearce had become a leading Methodist[10]. Worship continued at the Pippet Street chapel until 1818 when a much grander building was erected on Coppice Hill. (The old building, now 29 Market Street, today houses the Bradford on Avon Town Club.)

Wesley seems to have disliked the chapel as a place to preach; an entry in the Journal for 18 September 1764 records that "being determined to be no longer cooped up in the room at Bradford" he moved down to near the bridge (in fact, the market place then) where a "multitude" flocked to hear him. The following day he again preached for preference in the open, this time at Whitehill where "many had an opportunity of hearing who would not come to the room." Preaching in the open had its hazards, though, as the townsfolk were not always friendly. At Whitehill "the beasts of the people were tolerably quiet" till Wesley had nearly finished his sermon. "They then lifted up their voice, especially one, called a gentleman, who had filled his pocket with rotten eggs; but a young man coming unawares, clapped his hands on each side and mashed them all at once. In an instant he was perfume all over ..."

Worse had befallen travelling preacher William Hitchens, a dozen years before. He was thrust into the lock-up on the bridge[11] by the press-gang pending compulsory enlistment. Richard Pearce tried unsuccessfully to get him out on bail; the authorities said they would take his word for £10,000 (he must have been pretty well-off) but not for Hitchens. In the event the magistrates had to set Hitchens free when he was able to satisfy them that he owned property and was thus exempt from military service. Though uncomfortable his confinement was for

58

The 'blind house' (lock-up) on the town bridge, sometimes called 'the chapel'.
The pointed ribbed arch of the bridge is believed to be original (late Norman).

59

him rewarding; sleepless all night he preached to his guard of twelve soldiers who, as he said, "durst not leave.."[12]

On his early visits to Wesley sometimes stayed overnight at a boarding-house in Silver Street; the building is now three shops, Peter Dominic, A T Scrine and The Bouquet. There, he is said to have told his host, the beds were truly English; they had "no notion of giving out". (The old building today is egregious for its red brick frontage, perpetrated around the turn of the present century). On later visits Wesley enjoyed private hospitality, sometimes with Richard Pearce, sometimes with Anne Bailward, daughter-in-law of Constant. In September 1787 he stayed at Anne Bailward's for the last time. A year later he records her death: "good Mrs. Bailward ... after long struggling with a deep nervous disorder, which for a time depressed the mind as well as the body, the cloud removed; her load fell off, and her spirit joyfully returned to God."

In her will Anne Bailward left £80 for the benefit of the preachers at "Mr Wesley's Preaching House at Bradford" so long as they preached according to his doctrine.

On 18 September 1789 John Wesley, now 86, preached at the Bradford chapel, for the last time, to the "old, steady congregation; but many of them gone into a better world. Scarce any of the rich and honourable left; but it is enough that the gospel is preached to the poor." The following day, however, at Bath, there were "rich and honourable in abundance ... and seemed as attentive as colliers." Doubtless his thoughts went back to when, at nearby Kingswood a half century before, he had preached amid the slagheaps to the coalminers – and evangelical Methodism was born.

In the 40 years after Wesley's death in 1791 Methodism throve in Bradford as it did elsewhere. Nationwide, numbers went from 72,000 to 237,000. In Bradford the congregation outgrew the Pippet Street chapel and in 1818 a splendid new one was erected on Coppice Hill. Joseph Rawling, the Congregationalist minister, tells us in his autobiography (see above) that "in those days the rich and influential among the inhabitants of Bradford and vicinity did not consider themselves out of place or lowering their position to attend a Wesleyan ministry." Among these he numbered the Cams of Chantry House and John Smith, local attorney, whose daughter married (in 1805) distinguished churchman Dr Thomas Coke (1747-1814)[13].

Before the end of the last century Bradford ceased to be a leading centre and the decline continued in the present one. By the 1950s the congregation was not large enough to maintain the chapel and had to give up using it. In 1974 they crossed the town to join the United Reformed Church at St Margaret's Hill. The old chapel on Coppice Hill, now roofless, was sold to an adjoining owner who turned it into a private open-air swimming pool.

Two of Wesley's Bradford preachers achieved more than purely local renown in the church. Samuel Clark was only here for one year, sent in 1782 by Wesley himself at the age of 20. The young Irishman was, like Wesley, a brilliant, convincing and indefatigable speaker. Clearly a young man in a hurry, in his comparatively brief stay he preached over 500 sermons and married a Trowbridge girl, Mary Cooke. He then went off to a life of service to the movement acting several times as president of the Methodist Conference and achieving distinction as the author of a Bible commentary.

Quite different was Thomas Olivers who was in Bradford from 1749-53, in which time he went from convert to, from 1751, local preacher. He was self-educated – "a rough stick of wood" was how Wesley described him – who as well as earning his living six days a week as a mechanic (presumably on maintenance and repair in one or other of the clothing factories) dedicated the whole of Sunday, apart from two to three hours sleep from about 2 am, to his ministry. He would cover over 20 miles on foot in the course of visiting "a few poor people" from 6 – 7.00 am, preaching at different places at 1.00 pm and 5.00 pm then walking home so tired that he could scarce get over a stile or upstairs to bed.

In his spare time he wrote hymns, at least one of which *The God of Abraham praise* remains highly regarded.

In 1752 there was a serious smallpox epidemic in the town, and Olivers caught the disease and nearly died of it. He was grievously ill from October to New Year's Day, when he got out of bed for the first time to have the sheets changed. He tells how Richard Pearce, "that pattern of pastoral Christianity" engaged one of the best nurses in town, the chief apothecary and Dr Clark "the most experienced physician in all that country". (John Clark was the Quaker medical practitioner mentioned later.)

About this time Olivers received a small legacy with which he bought a horse and travelled about paying old debts. Finding on his return to Bradford that he had not enough money to repay Richard Pearce he sold horse and saddle, keeping the saddle-bags so that he could in future be his own pack-horse, only to find that Pearce refused to accept. In October, packing his books and and other few belongings in the saddle-bags and slinging them across his shoulders, he set off, at Wesley's behest, to preach the word in Cornwall. At Twerton, in Somerset, a Mr Bidgood gave him a horse. He was still riding it 25 years later. What a character!

The Coppice Hill chapel had an outpost at Bradford Leigh from 1822. It was registered as being at the house of James Hibberd, registrant James M Byron, Bradford Methodist minister. In 1892 a mission chapel was erected but it has been closed for many years.

Primitive Methodism

This group of Methodists seceded from the main church in 1810. Its appeal was to the poorest in the community. In 1825 "a building in the occupation of William Brown" was registered as their place of worship; the registrants were John Challinor and William Brown. In 1845 they registered "the chapel and premises now in the holding and occupation of William Crook, John Smith and others"; this presumably will have been the old chapel now converted to a dwelling-house at Sladesbrook. The church was never a strong one and ceased to exist as a separate body in 1932, when it was re-united with the Methodist Church.

The Quakers

By 1660 the Quakers of Bradford were worshipping regularly (and at that time illegally) just outside the town at Frankleigh – they called it Cumberwell – probably in the home of one of their number. It was in that year that a troop of cavalry broke into their meeting for worship and seized one of them, Robert Starr, whence he was taken to Sarum (Salisbury) and thrown into gaol.

By 1661 they had their own burial ground at Frankleigh and by 1676 owned a meeting house also. The meeting house was rebuilt by 1689 and Frankleigh continued as a place of worship and burial up to the end of the next century; the last burial there was in 1803. In 1813 it was sold for private occupation. It is now 119 Bath Road.

After the Toleration Act of 1689 it was lawful for Quakers and other Protestant dissenters to meet for worship in their own way and in 1718 a second Quaker meeting house was erected, this one in the town centre. It was a substantial building, seating 200, and cost £240 to build. With a burial ground[14] adjoining it stood in the area now bounded by St Margaret's Hall, the Riverside Restaurant and the houses in St Margaret's Street.

Between about 1670 and 1730 Bradford Quakers were numerous and influential. Thereafter membership declined and by the end of the eighteenth century both meeting houses were closed, the few remaining members transferring to Melksham.

The Bailward family were early Bradford Quakers. Constant Bailward (died 1744 and buried at Cumberwell) was a Quaker minister. She was born Constant Owen of Nailsworth and married John Bailward in 1713. Their son John, born 1715, in 1744 married Anne, daughter of Quaker linen draper Thomas Shewell of London[15]. But as time went on John and Anne drifted away from the Society of Friends. Anne seems to have hovered between Wesleyan Methodism (as we have seen) and the Anglican Church. In July 1780 she and her husband were recorded as having "seat rooms in the pews" of the parish church[16] (though the entry is crossed through); and a mural tablet in the parish church records Anne's death (on 25 July 1788). John was a trustee of the Methodist chapel. Their son Samuel married Anna Maria Stevens, a Methuen heiress and the Bailwards joined the ranks of the landed gentry, in due course to be celebrated as such in Burke's distinguished volumes.

The local doctor and surgeon in the late seventeenth/early eighteenth century, John Clark, (died 1726) was a Quaker. His son John (1684-1760) succeeded him in the practice; this was the Dr Clark who attended Thomas Olivers the Methodist preacher when he had small-pox. Another son was a "chymist". The elder John Clark had started life as a cabinet-maker in London; the events leading to his somewhat startling metamorphosis as a medical man are not on record. Perhaps it was that he found he had the gift of healing. He was clearly no charlatan and was held in high esteem by his fellow Quakers, for many years holding the position of clerk (chairman) of the group of Wiltshire meetings of which Bradford and Cumberwell (Frankleigh) were constituent members. His wife Anne (died 1745) was a minister, contemporary with Constant Bailward.

Some family names recur frequently in the early Quaker records. Examples are Baskerville (John, clothier, lived in Newtown, married Ann Webb also of Bradford in 1701), Grant (George, clothier, 1698), Moxham (John, died 1733), Noyes (Israel, clothier, 1723), Tyler (Charles of Bearfield, clothier, married Sarah Sanger in 1734). The

BRADFORD ON AVON PAST AND PRESENT

Knees of Trowbridge were members of the Bradford Meeting in the late eighteenth century.

A Quaker Meeting re-opened in Bradford in 1971 after a lapse of over 170 years. The old building of 1718 having fallen victim to the demolition men in the 1960s the Friends converted a private house in Whitehead's Lane. Unwittingly they were renewing a link with their past. Whitehead's Lane, so Canon Jones tells us[17] was named after Manasseh Whitehead – and Manasseh Whitehead was a seventeenth century Bradford Quaker.

NOTES

1. The wimple helps to date the effigy. Fashionable between the late twelfth century and the mid-fourteenth century it was a length of white linen or silk draped over the front of the neck and brought up under the chin with the ends pinned to the hair over the ears.

2. The *Bishop's Bible* was a fresh English translation which, in 1571, Queen Elizabeth's Archbishop of Canterbury, Matthew Parker, ordered to be used in all churches.

3. According to Robson's Commercial Directory for 1839 James Budget was in business in the Old Market as grocer, cheesemonger, tallow chandler and agent for the Standard of England Life Office. The shop was at what is now number 32, facing Coppice Hill. where the Old Market Hall stood (see description later); the business subsequently became Budgett and Jones.

4. Fuller later became chief architect to the Canadian government, He designed the Parliament building in Ottawa in 1859 and also the cathedral and parish church of St Johns, Antigua.

5. Conveniently tabulated in *Wiltshire Meeting House Certificates 1689-1852*, published by the Wiltshire Record Society, editor J H Chandler.

6. This Francis Yerbury (1638-1720) was the grandfather of the Francis Yerbury who in 1766, as noted elsewhere, invented and patented cassimere.

7. Flexman was the distinguished theologian, scholar and historian. Renowned for his painstaking accuracy, in 1770 he was appointed by the government to compile a general index to the journals of the House of Commons.

8. Selina Hastings (1707-1791), Countess of Huntingdon, was an early Wesley supporter who later branched out to develop Calvinistic Methodism for the upper classes. John Wesley records in his Journal that on 5 October 1766 he administered the sacrament in her chapel in Bath. Among those present were the Lord Chancellor, Lord Chatham, Lord Bedford, the Bishop of Londonderry and other distinguished persons. Horace Walpole was there; a letter of 10 October 1766 to his friend John Chute comments on the occasion.

9. In his journal Wesley calls her "Mrs. Ballard". The "Mrs. Bailward" he refers to later in the journal was Constant's daughter-in-law Anne (born Shewell) who married Constant's son John, in 1744. (see WRO 217/6, the marriage settlement document). Constant died later in the same year

CHURCHES, CHAPELS AND MEETING HOUSES

and was buried in the Quaker burial ground at Cumberwell. Constant's son John's name appears among the trustees of the chapel in 1767.

10. Not as paradoxical as might today appear. Water was unsafe and supply uncertain, beer comparatively wholesome and readily available. It was spirits, in particular gin, that were frowned upon; Hogarth's contemporary cartoons comparing the horrors of Gin Lane with the joys of prosperous Beer Street are *à propos*. Moderation was enjoined but total abstention was not practical policy till the next century.

11. The so-called "chapel on the bridge". It is a fairly typical Wiltshire blindhouse and dates from the seventeenth century. John Aubrey (1626-1697), probably writing from memory as he so often did, called it a chapel for mass. Aubrey was an amiable dilettante who dabbled in history and natural history and impoverished himself by a series of injudicious lawsuits. His descriptions tend to be inaccurate. As his is the only evidence we have of a chapel on the town bridge there is reason to doubt if the building that he saw, which must be the one we see now, was ever other than what it was a century later when the hapless Hitchens was incarcerated in it. Did the weather-vane with its fish, the classic Christian symbol, confuse Aubrey? In the previous century the more reliable and painstaking John Leland described the bridge but said nothing of any chapel. If there ever was one surely he, a clergyman, would have mentioned it.

The little building has certainly had its vicissitudes. According to Canon Jones it was used at times as a toll-house, to take tolls on beasts going to the Saturday market. On the Ordnance Survey Map of 1924 it is shown as a magazine (*viz* ammunition store). About that time it was repaired and restored by public subscription and handed over by Sir Charles Hobhouse, the then owner, to the Wiltshire County Council.

12. Hitchens retired from preaching the following year (1758); he had been "on the road" since 1745, and will have returned home to Cornwall. He was one of four brothers, all Methodist preachers, all much esteemed by John Wesley.

13. Anglican priest inclined towards Methodism who strove unsuccessfully to unite the two churches here and in North America, where he became a Methodist bishop. He was made Anglican bishop in India in 1813 but died on the voyage out.

14. Burials between 1700 and 1803, the last one that of Ann Eyles of Bradford, wife of James, aged 81. Now part of the car park.

15. WRO 217/6. A trustee of the marriage settlement was leading Quaker Ezekiel Dickinson of Monks, Corsham.

16. WRO 242 77/1

17. WAM xx p.306: *A Walk through Bradford on Avon*.

5 SCHOOLS

Right up to the early eighteenth century the notion that schooling was proper for other than the upper classes was alien to English thought. In the Middle Ages, and for some time after, such scraps of elementary education as were occasionally thrown to the poor came from the established church. As in the country at large so in Bradford. We have seen that Horton's Chantry included a school of sorts and we know from the records that in 1548 William Furbner the chantry priest was, single-handed, conducting it and that the vicar was expected to train children as choristers. Such instruction as was given will have had a bias to religious doctrine, in particular that of the established (then, of course, Roman Catholic) church. When the chantry was closed and its property seized the school continued for a while, still under Furbner, doctrine suitably modified no doubt. It was now supported by an annual grant from the Crown of ten pounds twelve shillings and sevenpence. But a few years later, in 1559, Furbner having died or given up (he would be about 67 then) the authorities of the city of Salisbury seized the opportunity to get their hands on the money by persuading Queen Elizabeth that education was wasted on a town like Bradford and it would therefore be better paid to them. Thereafter, for about a century and a half, the town was without a school of any kind.

The Free Grammar School
In the reign of Queen Anne (1702-1714) the Church of England authorities, feeling threatened by the success of the schools being established by the dissenting sects, decided to set up free schools in

competition to "educate the children of the poor in reading, writing, moral discipline and the principles of the Church of England." At the same time they tried, by the Schism Act of 1713, to suppress the dissenters' schools by making them unlawful. In this they failed. The dissenters refused to obey the law and in 1718 succeeded in getting it repealed.

On 17 January 1712, the vicar of Bradford, John Rogers, set up a school for boys of the parish in the building we now know as the Saxon church. The project proved a success, so much so that five years later it was put on a sound footing by Ann Wright (formerly the Hon. Lady Ann Powlett) and her husband the Reverend Nathan Wright, the then lords of the manor. "For the encouragement of learning and good manners within the parish of Bradford" they made over the building to William Methuen and eight others in trust to assure the school's continuance.

From then till the latter part of the nineteenth century the school continued to receive much local support. A clergyman, Edward Dike, gave £50 and another £50 was subscribed by local well-wishers. In about 1727 Francis Smith, a Bradford maltster, bequeathed the then substantial sum of £250 to be invested and the income made available for educating ten more poor Bradford children there. Edward Wadman was a supporter in the 1740s. In 1805 John Strawbridge of Bradford bequeathed £400; in 1850 John Bubb bequeathed £50 to educate four more poor Bradford boys; and in 1860 Hannah Smith left £50, the income from it to be used to augment the master's stipend.

What the school was like in the nineteenth century we know from the Charity Commission reports of 1834 and 1901. The master in 1834 was James Grist, who had been appointed in 1819. His salary was £40 a year and he lived on the premises rent and rates free. Instruction was in reading, writing and arithmetic only. There were 50 pupils. Of these, 32 were nominated by the trustees to receive free tuition but had to pay one shilling and eightpence a quarter for writing-books, pens and ink. The remainder paid fees, but all received the same instruction and received it on the same footing. Because places were much sought after the maximum stay permitted was three years.

In 1834 the commissioners had described the building as being in a very dilapidated state. Little seems to have been done to remedy this, to judge by its condition when in 1874, as described elsewhere, the school trustees swapped it for Old Church House (now in part Trinity Church

Hall and in part a Freemasons' Lodge) where the cross-wing at the north end of the building became the schoolroom, the rest of the building being rented off as cottages.

By 1901 the school is beginning to sound a bit like Dotheboys Hall. There is still only one master, Frederick William Cowlishaw, who succeeded John Thornton Butt in 1875. Single-handed, in one "long narrow high room", he teaches 60 boys of between the ages of 7 and 14-plus. There is no playground. Basic teaching is still the three Rs, but between 30 and 40 boys do either history or geography as well. In addition 40 boys take drawing at an extra charge of seven shillings and

Old Church House. From 1874 to 1903 it was the free grammar school. It is now in part Trinity Church hall and in part Freemasons' Lodge.

sixpence a year. All do singing and "drill" (physical exercises). It all seems very inadequate and yet Mr Cowlishaw is able to tell the commissioners that over the past three years 25 boys have entered the Civil Service (Post Office and Customs and Excise) by competitive examination and 54 have gone straight from school to become railway staff. We learn that Mr. Cowlishaw is a certificated teacher and a member of the College of Preceptors. Clearly he is no Wackford Squeers, however adverse his circumstances.

In 1899, largely as a result of misgivings which that distinguished resident Lord Edmond Fitzmaurice MP (1846-1935), (later Lord Fitzmaurice of Leigh), expressed about the school a public enquiry was held. The Hon. W N Bruce, an Assistant Commissioner under the Endowed Schools Acts, who conducted it, reported unfavourably. He found the school below standard, its finances mismanaged and its accounts badly kept. He commented that the 60 pupils were mainly sons of farmers and small tradesmen and were said to be of a different class from those using the public elementary schools. The Charity Commissioners accordingly recommended closure. They saw, they said, little likelihood of the establishment being run so as to offer any real educational advantage to the poor which was what the founders had intended. The trustees resisted, but in vain, and the school was closed in 1903.

National Schools and British Ones

By the early nineteenth century there was a growing awareness that England was falling behind the rest of Western Europe in the matter of education. In changing times it was felt that all children, however humble their background, should receive a measure of schooling. Progress was hampered by sectarian rivalry. For a long time the Church of England was dominant both at primary level and at the universities of Oxford and Cambridge from which, until 1871, non-Anglicans were barred. In 1807 progressives from both church and chapel, aiming to bridge sectarian differences in the interests of public education, formed the British and Foreign School Society. The policy was to set up schools, to be called British Schools, where the religious instruction would be non-denominational. In 1811 the Anglicans, no doubt feeling threatened, formed the National Society for the Education of the Poor according to the Principles of the Church of England to establish what they called National Schools. In these schools children would be taught

Lord Fitzmaurice of Leigh in old age.

not only the three Rs but also the catechism (sometimes summarised by the disrespectful as "God bless the squire and his relations and keep us all in our proper stations"). They would also receive weekly visits by the vicar or his curate to ensure that religious instruction was sound.

In Bradford a British School was opened in the disused Quaker Meeting House. Quaker records show that the building was let, free of charge, as a school for poor children as early as 1806. In 1817 there was a formal agreement with Charles Cadby and others for the premises to be used as a British School for boys. The building stood in the area, now part of a car park, bounded by a dye-shop (now St Margaret's Hall), a house belonging to Charles Timbrell (now the Riverside Restaurant) and the house now called Westbury House. The school was popular; in 1830 average attendance was 140 to 200.

In 1836 the National Society and local Anglicans opened a rival establishment in Church Street which they called Trinity Church National School. This also was successful; in 1859 there were 50 to 60 boys and 80 to 90 girls. There was one master and one mistress. After 1880 when elementary education was made compulsory numbers increased. In 1896 the school was enlarged to provide places for 157 boys, 168 girls and 204 infants. A new building was added on an adjacent site, with access from Newtown.

In 1847 a second National School called Christchurch School was opened at Mount Pleasant. When it came to the establishment of a Church of England school it was customary for a local landowner to donate the land on which it was to be built. Sir John Hobhouse, the Lord of the Manor, duly obliged and Captain S H Palairet paid for the building. With the continuing support of the local moneyed Christchurch School flourished. In 1878 an infants' school was erected on an adjoining site given by Miss Isabella Poynder (died 1880) of Leigh House. Miss Poynder had always taken a great interest in the school and she was accustomed to giving the pupils a treat from time to time. We know, for example, that in June 1867 she entertained 150 children to tea in her garden followed by singing, dancing to the violin, football and other delights. Then, children dismissed, the master and mistress (Caleb Bryant and his wife Mercy) and the pupil teachers stayed on for supper. We also know that in January 1869 she gave 167 scholars a hot dinner of roast beef, roast mutton, three kinds of vegetables, bread, plum pudding, mince pies and beer. Ten of her servants carved for and waited on the children. Miss Poynder would also give money prizes for outstanding work. For boys the prizes were for handwriting, arithmetic and mapping, for the girls needlework.

The British Schools (in 1860 one for girls had been started in Church Street) enjoyed no such support. The boys' school went gradually downhill in increasingly decrepit surroundings. The final indignity came in 1880 when the building was declared by the Board of Education to be unfit for its purpose. The *Trowbridge Advertiser* of 25 September 1880 quoted the inspector's report "...ventilation most imperfect- ...smoke from neighbouring factory...effluvia from a rank and confined stable...position gloomy and depressing...no playground except the factory yard..." The press report added that leading Nonconformists in the town were "determined that unsectarian education shall not cease to be provided." It so happened that about this time the Nonconformists had built in Mason's Lane (on the site of a weaving workshop destroyed by fire in July 1869) a school for girls and infants. Known as the Undenominational School it will have succeeded the one in Church Street. With the closure of the building which had housed the boys' school the boys were transferred to this one.

The twentieth century saw the demise of the old sectarian rivalries, though they died hard. The Undenominational School in Mason's Lane closed in the late 1920s and its pupils were transferred to a newly built "council" (*viz* non-sectarian) school in Trowbridge Road, now (1988) relocated and redesignated Fitzmaurice Primary School, with access from Frome Road. (The school building in Mason's Lane later became private houses, numbers 10, 10a and 11).

Christchurch Church of England School, now redesignated Christ-church Church of England Controlled Primary School, continues in new buildings on land adjacent to the old buildings, with access from Sladesbrook.

Trinity School became, in the late 1940s, Trinity Secondary Modern School which in 1980, in accordance with national educational policy, merged with Fitzmaurice Grammar School to form St Laurence Voluntary Controlled Comprehensive School in new buildings in Ashley Road; now redundant, the 1836 building in Church Street was converted into flats and the 1896 one demolished to make way for sheltered housing, the Ropewalk development.

Fitzmaurice Grammar School
Lord Edmond Fitzmaurice, whose doubts about the value of the Free School in Old Church House eventually led to its closure in 1903, played a leading part in the establishment of the County Technical and Secondary School, later called the Fitzmaurice Grammar School in his honour. The first headmaster was John Crompton M.A. a mathematics exhibitioner of Jesus College, Oxford. The building was erected in Junction Road (architect J B Silcock) and opened in 1897. It continued in use until the Grammar School ceased to exist in its own right in 1980. It then came under threat of demolition for redevelopment; but local opinion in favour of its conservation prevailed and it is now (1988) about to become part of a sheltered housing scheme.
The new school had everything going for it. Where Mr Cowlishaw

John Crompton, first headmaster of Fitzmaurice Grammar School, in 1910.

73

had been, with inadequate financial backing, coping single-handedly with 60 boys of various ages and abilities in one room (yet still getting acceptable results), the County School had spacious purpose-built classrooms, a vigorous and highly qualified headmaster, a headmistress (Miss Blake) and a staff of four full-time and three visiting teachers. Not surprisingly, from the time the rival establishment opened pupils had been drifting away from Mr Cowlishaw's school; the remnant will have transferred with the closure in 1903. In that year the County School had 57 pupils of whom 20 were girls. Most of the pupils were of the white collar worker class, though one boy's father (as noted in the Board of Education school inspectors' report) was "professional and independent". Eight fathers were farmers and seven were artisans (skills unspecified). Fees were four pounds ten shillings a year.

Private Schools

A number of small private educational establishments have been run in Bradford at various locations at various times by private individuals. There was one for ten children in what is now St Mary's Chapel, Tory, according to the Rev. J Cox's *Magna Britannica* published between 1720 and 1731. In Pippett Street (now Market Street) in 1841 Miss Fanny Wilshire conducted an infants' school; she also took bookings for the coaches. We know of one at the Chantry; Charles Rawling's *Pictorial Guide* published in 1887 records that a Dr Knight had been master there and so had the Reverend Charles Thring. Thring, a curate at the parish church, had previously taught at Uppingham School, where his brother was headmaster. He lived on the premises with his wife Lydia and their family of five daughters and three sons. In 1893 there was a "Young Gentlemen's Boarding School" at Avon Villas, Principal S S Lane Esq. B.A.; a "High Class School for Girls" at Avon House, Principal Miss E F Watkins; and one "Young Ladies' Seminary" at 6 St Margaret's Place, which was run by Mrs and Miss Vernon and another at Albert Terrace run by the Misses Harman. From 1895 to 1932 Miss Mabel Cockrom and her brother kept a "Preparatory School for Young Ladies and Gentlemen under 12 years of age" at 28 St Margaret's Street.

Outside the town centre there was a private school at Pottick's House on the Bath road; Kelly's Directory for Hampshire, Wiltshire and Dorset for 1859 shows that Alfred H Mansell was then running a "Gentlemen's Boarding School" there. Also on the Bath Road, Frankleigh House was being advertised in the Trowbridge Advertiser in 1879

Frankleigh House, now The Old Ride Preparatory School for Boys.

as "the Grammar School". Later on, still used as a private school, it was renamed Kingswell Court. It now houses the one private school left in Bradford, Old Ride Preparatory School for Boys. The building has early seventeenth century origins with a major extension in 1848, see next chapter under "Frankleigh House".

6 THE BUILDINGS

The toune self of Bradeford standith on the clining of a slaty rokke
...The toune is made al of stone ...
John Leland

I FINE HOUSES AND DISTINGUISHED OCCUPANTS
Three things in Bradford impressed Leland in 1540; the predominance
of cloth manufacture; the wealthy families, enriched, like the Halls, by
inherited land or, like the Hortons, by industrial enterprise; and the
splendid stone houses.

THE HALL
The building that Leland called "a pratie stone house at the este end of
the towne" will most probably have been a typical hall of the Middle
Ages. In its place, some half century after his visit, the present building
was erected, probably by John Hall, doubtless larger and grander than
its predecessor and certainly Bradford's most distinguished existing
building.

But it was very nearly lost to the town. In 1805 it was sold to Thomas
Divett, clothier, who erected a factory alongside called Kingston Mill.
In about 1836 it was leased to Samuel Pitman, Trowbridge clothier,
(father of Sir Isaac Pitman, inventor of the shorthand system called by
his name). In 1848 the house, by that time in a state of near-dereliction,
was restored by Stephen Moulton to what we see today. (The building
contractor was James Long who also built the town hall – now the
Church of St Thomas More – and the bank premises in Church Street
formerly the North Wilts Bank, now Lloyd's). Re-roofed in 1981 by Dr

The Hall, Bradford on Avon

77

Alex Moulton, the present owner, the house is safe for the foreseeable future.

The Hall was paid a nice compliment by the French in 1900; at the Paris exhibition they reproduced the south front for the English pavilion erected in honour of the visit of the Prince of Wales (later Edward VII).

The Hall Family

The Halls were a prominent Bradford land-owning family from at least the mid-thirteenth century, the family name being written down then and later variously as "Hall", "at Halle", "de Aula" and (by John Leland)"de la Sale", all meaning the same thing, *viz* "from the Hall"- the big house. John Hall founded the Hall's Almshouses in Frome Road and his arms may be seen on the building with the date AD 1700 and the inscription *Deo et pauperibus* (for God and the poor). John Hall left no male heir and on his death in 1711 the family name died out in Bradford.

Hall left all his property to Rachel Baynton, who, though she had been baptised (in April 1695) as the daughter of Thomas and Elizabeth Baynton, is said to have been his natural daughter. Through her marriage to William Pierrepont, son and heir of the Marquis of Dorchester, who later became the first Duke of Kingston, the Hall passed to their son Evelyn, second and last Duke of Kingston. It was Evelyn whom Elizabeth Chudleigh, already married to Augustus Hervey, Earl of Bristol, bigamously married in 1769. Elizabeth succeeded to the estate when Evelyn died in 1773 and it was then that the truth about her other marriage became known, ferreted out by disappointed heirs. Elizabeth's five day trial in the House of Lords in April 1776 was, not surprisingly, a *cause célèbre*. Although she was found guilty she went unpunished and the property was held to be hers inalienably.[1]

The Moulton Family

Stephen Moulton (1794-1880) was born in Whorlton, County Durham. In 1827 he married Elizabeth Riche and subsequently settled in New York. In 1847 they returned to England to settle in Bradford on Avon, where, as we have seen, Stephen set up as a manufacturer of rubber. Three sons, Alexander (died 1885), Horatio (1837-1893) and John (1839-1925) in due course joined their father in the firm. Alexander succeeded him and was head of the firm for the five years till his death. In 1891 the brothers Horatio and John joined forces with their father's old friend George Spencer to form George Spencer, Moulton and Co. Horatio became chairman and on his death was succeeded by John.

The family have a distinguished record of public service and conservation in the town. John served with distinction on District and County Councils and was High Sheriff for the county in 1917. With Lord Edmond Fitzmaurice he was a major donor of the public baths and pleasure ground on the south bank of the river, now, alas, become a mere public car park; the iron railings on the river side bearing the initial letters JM in the form of a monogram are all that remain of a once pleasant haven.

The last bearer of the family name still living in the town is Dr Alex Moulton, great-grandson of Stephen. Dr Moulton, who describes himself as "an innovating engineer" is best known as the inventor of the Moulton bicycle; but he is distinguished also as the inventor of *Flexitor*, a type of trailer suspension still produced at Bradford. Rubber suspension designed by him was used in the British Leyland "Mini" and his *Hydrolastic* suspension was used for the Austin/Morris 1100/1300 range. Later on his *Hydragas* suspension (which replaced rubber suspensions by gas-sprung ones) were adopted by British Leyland for the Austin Metro and Austin Ambassador. *Hydragas* received the Queen's Award to Industry in 1967.

WESTWOOD MANOR

Almost nothing remains in Bradford itself of the "very fair house of the building of one Horton" which John Leland saw and noted. It is now the rear part of the building called Abbey House in Church Street. The building now called Trinity Church Hall which Thomas Horton built has, however, survived and externally at least is very much as Leland will have seen it.

But Thomas Horton also owned Westwood Manor House (about $1\frac{1}{2}$ miles south- west of Bradford) from about 1513. The original building, erected before 1400, had been a modest farmhouse on land held under the Priory of Winchester. In 1480 Thomas Culverhouse, owner then, enlarged it substantially. Thomas Horton enlarged it still more. Clearly to be included in his contribution is the present dining-room. On the left and right spandrels of the fireplace are carved respectively the initials T and H. In the bedroom above the dining-room the oriel window contains a roundel of stained glass with a rebus formed by the three letters HOR over a barrel or tun. (This is a copy of the original which was removed and placed in the church just before 1900).

Westwood Manor is now National Trust property.

The Horton Family

The Hortons claimed descent from Roger de Horton, Justice of Cheshire in 1428. They are said to have been drawn to the West of England by the prospect of riches from the clothing industry. If so they were not disappointed; by the early sixteenth century they owned land at Trowbridge, North Bradley, Southwick, Westbury, Rode, Frome, Wolverton, Bradford, Westwood, Iford, Farleigh, Hinton, Chippenham, Foxham, Sevington, Tilshead, Cheverill, Cricklade, Corsley, Tellisford and Freshford. Later on they were to do well out of Henry VIII's dissolution of the monasteries.[2] Thomas Horton (died 1530), the Bradford benefactor, included in his property Westwood Manor and Iford Manor and built the substantial house in Bradford in which he lived. Thomas was a great churchman. His Bradford home was as near to the parish church as he could get it: "... at the north est part by the chirch" as John Leland observed. He built the church hall. And to the parish church he added, in what is now the north aisle, a chantry chapel; the brass recording this, formerly set in the chapel floor, is now on the east wall of the north aisle. At Westwood either he or his nephew Thomas built the church tower; the initials TH are above the entrance. In his will he left property to Hinton Charterhouse Priory.

Thomas Horton died childless and his property went to his nephew of the same name. This Thomas seems to have moved out of Bradford, probably to Iford; when Leland visited the town (in the early 1540s) he noted that "one Lucas, a clothier, now dwelleth in Horton's house." (Thomas's wife Mary's maiden name had been Lucas so the property was evidently still in the family). Nephew Thomas died in 1549 and in his will he left, among other estate, "all the lands ... acquired from King Henry VIII". He had evidently been on very good terms with that monarch – as noted earlier, when his uncle's chantry was dissolved he had succeeded in acquiring some of the chantry endowment. Thomas's daughter Alice married into the Yerbury family, as to whom see later.

PRIORY HOUSE, Market Street

At the time of Leland's visit in 1540 another fine house in the town was the one belonging to Thomas Rogers, Serjeant-at-Law. Priory House in Market Street is lineally descended from the house probably built by him in about 1460. Hardly anything remains of the original building except perhaps the wall on to Market Street which, as can readily be seen, was once the outside wall of part of a building.

From 1657 the Bradford house was owned by the Methuen family. John Methuen (died 1706) who, as described elsewhere, negotiated, as ambassador to Portugal, the important Methuen Treaty of 1703, will have been born there.

The Methuen family were owners until 1763 when they sold to the Tugwell family. In 1811 Mawbey Tugwell (died 1815) sold the property to fellow-clothier John Saunders, who added the ktchen wing – which is all that remains today of the building he knew.

John was succeeded by his son Thomas Hosier Saunders, partner in the clothing firm of Saunders, Fanner and Saunders[3] who in turn was succeeded by his son Thomas Bush Saunders, who departed from family tradition and became a barrister. Up to that time the property had been known as Methuen's but Thomas Bush Saunders seems to have decided to call it The Priory even before he leased it to a detachment of the Sisters of the Holy Trinity for a few years in the 1850s. (In the 1871 census return it is called the *Old* Priory.)

When Thomas Bush Saunders died in 1894 the property went to his daughter Mrs Collett. Within the next half century it changed hands twice more, in 1930 and 1937. In 1937 it had been unoccupied and on the market for some time. The estate of some 14) acres was therefore broken up into lots and sold for development and in the following year almost all the ancient house was pulled down.

The splendid tulip tree which John Saunders planted remains to this day. (When Canon Jones's history was revised by John Beddoe in 1907 a second one was extant).

The stone barn which formed part of the property until 1937 belongs now to the Bradford on Avon Preservation Trust.

The site itself may well be one of great antiquity. A modest exploratory dig in 1978 by Mrs Pamela Slocombe revealed, besides medieval and possibly Saxon sherds, Roman artefacts consisting of a piece of combed box tile and a sherd of grey hard fabric, with single line incised decoration. Roman coins were found in the garden in 1818.

Above: *Priory House, late Georgian extension of the medieval mansion.*
Below: *Clothing magnate Humphrey Tugwell (1704-75) and his wife Elizabeth (1711-1801) 'constant and liberal benefactress of the poor lived in the old house.' (Thomas Gainsborough's portraits are reproduced here by kind permission of Sir Mervyn Medlycott, Bt, their descendant and courtesy of The Paul Mellon Centre for Studies in British Art).*

Thomas Rogers (fl.1460)

Thomas Rogers was a serjeant-at-law, a legal bigwig appointed personally by the sovereign. Together with the extensive land-ownership at Bradford, Cumberwell and Holt, Thomas will have been a man of considerable consequence nationally as well as locally[4]. Thomas's grandson Sir Edward Rogers (died 1582) held the even more important office of Comptroller of the Household to Queen Elizabeth.

John Methuen (c 1650-1706)

John Methuen was Member of Parliament for Devizes from 1690 to 1705 and was envoy to Portugal in 1691 and 1702 and ambassador in 1703, the year in which he negotiated the famous Methuen Treaty. He was Chancellor of Ireland for seven years.

Paul Methuen (1672-1757)

John Methuen's son Paul succeeded his father as ambassador to Portugal in 1706 and remained in post till 1708. He then became Member of Parliament for Devizes. He held office in government on and off until 1730. He died unmarried and was buried near his father in Westminster Abbey. He left £250,000 of which £50,000 was in gold coins, found in sealed bags in the house. Horace Walpole called him "a dull, formal, romantic braggadochio". But John Gay wrote of him:

Methuen of sincerest mind
As Arthur grave, as soft as womankind.

The town of Methuen, Massachusetts, was named after him.

Thomas Bush Saunders (1808-94)

Thomas Bush Saunders is remembered as the restorer of the chapel of St Mary, Tory (John Leland's "chapelle on the highest place of the towne") which, when he bought it in 1869, was little more than a ruin. Saunders was a barrister of Lincoln's Inn and Queen's Counsel but by 1871 was no longer in practice. In retirement he was a senior magistrate and chairman of the Bradford on Avon District Council.

CHANTRY HOUSE, Church Street

When Thomas Horton founded his chantry in 1524 in what is now the north aisle of the parish church he provided also the "mantyon house of the chantry". Much enlarged it has come down to us, its name essentially intact after a varied career as private house, clothier's business premises and private school. It is now divided into two private houses called respectively Chantry House and Little Chantry.

Little Chantry is what we see as we walk past the parish church on the left. Chantry House, to the rear, contains the original building, a feature of which is a built-in stone tank constantly replenished with fresh water by a rivulet flowing through; this will have been a kind of larder of fresh fish for the table. Over this is a small room said to have been a priest's room or place of concealment.

In 1598 King Edward VI dissolved the chantry and sold the house to Thomas Horton, a nephew of the founder of it (see above). It remained a private house up to 1794 when it was leased to John Yerbury, clothier, as his home and business premises. Yerbury added a factory building and purchased adjoining land giving access to the river, which he used thereafter to transport goods to and from Avoncliff where his brother-in-law John Moggridge had recently built a factory and workers' accommodation (now The Old Court).

The property stayed domestic/industrial for the next half century. It was used as such successively by Ebenezer Brown (from 1807 to 1810) and Samuel Mundy and Co. (up to about 1842), when Samuel Mundy, like so many other Bradford clothiers at that time, went out of business. The factory was pulled down and the house was used for some years as a small private school. From 1891 it was the home of John Beddoe, a private house once again.

Samuel Cam and the Hobhouse Family

Samuel Cam (died 1792) lived at Chantry House from 1741, having bought it when the previous owner, Edward Thresher died. From humble origins Cam had grown rich in the clothing trade. His only child, Charlotte, married, in 1785, Benjamin Hobhouse (1757-1831); they had three sons and one daughter.

Charlotte and her father were Presbyterians with, like so many other members of the congregation at the Grove Chapel (of which Samuel was a generous benefactor) a marked leaning to Unitarianism. Charlotte, as soon as her firstborn little son John Cam Hobhouse was old enough, sent

Chantry House

him to the school at Bristol conducted by eminent Unitarian preacher and schoolmaster John Prior Estlin.

Charlotte died in 1791 and her father died the following year, whereupon Benjamin Hobhouse became owner and, for a short while, occupier. He kept up his Bradford connexions but his ambitions were in national politics. These ambitions were realised; in due course he became Chief Secretary of the Board of Control for India. He was created baronet in 1812.

John Cam Hobhouse (1786-1869) also made politics his career, but not until he was well into his thirties. Perhaps a strict Puritan upbringing plus intimate friendship with the raffish Lord Byron[5] from their time together at Cambridge University was the explosive mixture which governed his anti-establishment stance for many years and eventually landed him in gaol for a brief spell; for his openly expressed approval of Napoleon Bonaparte and his attacks on the French monarchy and British government policy he was sent to Newgate on 14 December 1819 for alleged breach of parliamentary privilege. Luckily for him, the old parliament was dissolved at the end of February 1820, whereupon he was released and at the ensuing election the tables were turned and he became a member of the new one. Thereafter he pursued an extremely successful career, becoming in turn Secretary for War, Chief Secretary for Ireland and President of the Board of Control. In 1851 he was created Baron Broughton of Broughton Gifford.

Benjamin's second son, Benjamin, was killed at Waterloo.

Henry William Hobhouse (1791-1868) was Member of Parliament for Hereford. He was also a partner, with his father and Charles Phillott and Charles Lowder, in the local private banking firm of Hobhouse, Phillott and Lowder, which had branches in Bath and Church Street, Bradford on Avon. He also had links with India, having been employed there for a time by the East India Company.

The present holder of the baronetcy, who is also the Lord of the Manor of Bradford, is Sir Charles Chisholm Hobhouse (born 1906), of Monkton Farleigh Manor.

John Beddoe (1826-1911)

John Beddoe was born at Bewdley in Worcestershire. He was in medical practice in Bristol from 1857 to 1890 with a short break when he served as an army doctor in Turkey during the war in the Crimea. He retired to Bradford in 1891. In 1907 he re-published "with notes and continuation" Canon Jones's classic history of the town, first published in the Wilts Archaeological Magazine in 1859, together with an article on the Hall by Canon Jackson first published in the same magazine in 1854.

Beddoe was a keen anthropologist, particularly interested in head shapes and colour of eyes and hair, on which subjects he wrote a number of articles in learned publications. He was a Fellow of the Royal Society and an active member of the Anthropological Institute and of the Anthropological Society of London, on both of which bodies he served as president.

CHURCH HOUSE, Church Street

This handsome Georgian house was from 1821 to 1842 the banking premises of Hobhouse, Phillott and Lowder. The owner was then Sir Benjamin Hobhouse; the bankers were Sir Benjamin himself, his second son Henry William, Charles Phillott and Charles Lowder. When the bank failed in 1841 the property was bought by Thomas Wheeler who leased the ground floor to the North Wilts Bank who later moved into new premises adjoining, now Lloyd's Bank.

Church House, one-time bank premises of Hobhouse, Phillot and Lowder.

WESTBURY HOUSE, St Margaret's Street

Westbury House, formerly Bethell House, was built in the early eighteenth century.

In 1791 it was the scene of an ugly riot (described elsewhere) by unemployed cloth-workers against the then owner, Phelps, a clothier who had introduced machinery into his factory. Not long after this Dr Bethell, a physician, became the owner. He was the father of Richard Bethell, first Lord Westbury. Subsequent owners were George Spencer, of Spencer, Moulton and Co, and Charles Adye, County Architect. From 1911 to 1973 the house was the offices of the Bradford Urban District Council. It has since been converted into flats.

Richard Luttrell Pilkington Bethell, 1st Lord Westbury (1800-73) was born in Westbury House. He was educated at Bristol and Wadham College, Oxford, which he entered at the age of 14. He took his degree at the age of 18 and was made a fellow of his college.

In 1823 he became a barrister and rapidly built up a first-class practice. In 1851 he became Liberal Member of Parliament for Aylesbury and in the following year was knighted and made Solicitor General in the government of Lord Aberdeen. Later he became Attorney General and in 1861 Lord Chancellor, when he was elevated to the peerage as Lord Westbury of Westbury.

In 1865 he fell from grace a little following a scandal in connexion with Leeds Bankruptcy Court. Though he was not personally involved a motion of censure in the House of Commons declared him negligent in not having detected what was going on. In consequence he had to resign, though, his character not in question, he continued to sit as one of the Lords of Appeal.

Westbury House

Druce's Hill House

DRUCE'S HILL HOUSE, Church Street

This attractive house was described, in a survey of 1738-40 (in the Dean and Chapter's records in the Bristol Record Office), as "new-built". It then belonged to Anthony Druce, who came of a long line of Druces whose name appears, from the mid-sixteenth century on, in parish church registers, lists of churchwardens and in various property transactions. (Canon Jones, incidentally, writes of an Anthony and a William Druce as Quakers but their names do not appear as such in any of the Quaker records in the County Record Office.)

Anthony Druce was not owner for long. The house passed out of his possession when he became bankrupt in about 1740[6] and it is pretty certain that he, at least, was not a Quaker. If he had been, his bankruptcy would certainly have been recorded and deplored in the Quaker minute book of the day – and it is not. (Among eighteenth century Quakers failure in business was tantamount to sin; such a rare event was always closely investigated and evidence of negligence or culpability could result in expulsion from membership). But later in the century the house came into the possession of the Bailward family, who, as we have seen, *were* Quakers and this may be what the Canon had in mind. The house remained in the Bailwards' ownership until well into the last century.

KINGSTON PLACE, formerly The Vicarage

John Leland noted the existence of a vicarage "at the west ende of the chirch" and the present building, largely Victorian, doubtless occupies the same site and includes some, at least, of the original building. It was the home of the celebrated Canon W H R Jones when he was vicar from 1851 till his death in 1885.

Canon William Henry Rich Jones (1817-85)

Canon Jones is remembered for his discovery of the Saxon church, as described earlier, for his work on the Domesday Book and for his classic history of the town, first published in the form of articles in the Wiltshire Archaeological Magazine by the Wiltshire Archaeological and Natural History Society, of which he was vice president.

Jones was born at Blackfriars and educated at King's College, London, and Magdalen Hall (now Hertford College) Oxford, where he won the prize for Sanskrit. Before his appointment to Bradford in 1851 he had been Rector of the church of St Martin-in-the-Fields and of St James's, Shoreditch. He died suddenly at the vicarage on 28 October 1885.

ORPIN'S HOUSE and Edward Orpin

The attractive small house in Church Street, which was owned by Edward Orpin (died 1781) and is believed to have been designed by him was built some time after 1760. An unusual feature is the pair of round "bottle glass" windows set in the wall (they give light in two closets), the aim being, it is said, to reduce liability to the window tax in force at the time.

Orpin is remembered as the subject of Thomas Gainsborough's portrait *The Parish Clerk*. He was, in fact, a borough official – Coroner of the Market[7], a man of authority in his field. His acquaintance with Thomas Gainsborough, however, seems to have been slight. Although Charles Rawling states, in his *1887 Pictorial Guide*, that when Gainsborough and his friend the actor Garrick lived in Bath they used to visit Orpin in Bradford on Avon, an article by W J Loftie in *The Architectural Review* of February 1905 suggests otherwise.[8]

Orpin's House

Canon Jones

BRADFORD ON AVON TOWN CLUB, 29 Market Street

This was the site of the *Maidenhead Inn*, malthouse and brewhouse from some time before 1611. In 1755 Methodist innkeeper Richard Pearce (see above) bought the property, renovated the inn, (the front elevation dates from then) and demolished the malthouse to make way for a Methodist chapel. The chapel continued in use until the opening of a larger one on Coppice Hill in 1818. In the 1840s the building was taken over by Joseph Rawling for his printing business and Joseph's son Charles continued there from his father's death in 1866 to his own in 1903.

In 1903 John Moulton bought the property on behalf of the Conservative Club, refurbished it and in the following year leased it to them as their new premises. On John Moulton's death in 1925 the property was bought by a newly-formed non-political social club, the present Bradford on Avon Club.

Joseph Rawling (1792-1866)

Joseph Rawling, besides being the town's printer was also, from 1852, the postmaster. As noted elsewhere, he was also minister of Bearfield Congregational Church.

Rawling was born and grew up in Exeter. As a boy he was converted to Methodism and became a lay preacher at the age of 18. He worked as a printer, first in Bristol, where in 1815 he married, then in Bath.

Shortly after his grandfather's death in 1816 he came to Bradford and set up on his own as a printer and bookseller, at first with small success. Business improved after 1820 following a move to the building in Church Street now called Old Bank House. Trade directories show that he was trading as printer, bookseller, stationer, account book manufacturer and agent for the Sun, Fire and Eagle Life Office "and all the London newspapers". The 1841 tithe map shows that in that year he was still trading at the Church Street premises and that he was also owner of what is now 6 Pippet Buildings. Shortly afterwards he moved to 29 Market Street. His post office was next door (now number 28).

The Rawling family business printed, published and sold a wide range of good quality material from handbills to bound books. In 1865 Joseph Rawling wrote an autobiography which he printed, published and sold at the Pippet Street premises.

There is a stained glass window to his memory in the parish church.

BELCOMBE COURT, WELLCLOSE HOUSE and the Yerburys

A characteristic of the seventeenth, eighteenth and nineteenth centuries was the growing concentration of wealth in the hands of certain families, very often through intermarriage between members of the same nonconformist religious persuasion. Some of the fine houses that have come down to us were built or extended by such families, among whom we can include the Presbyterian Yerburys.

Belcombe Court stands on Belcombe Road some three quarters of a mile to the west of the town centre. John Yerbury (1678-1728) built on the site, which he acquired in 1722, a clothier's house and factory combined, a fairly typical arrangement in those days. He called it Bellcombe Brook House. In 1734 John's son Francis (1706-1778) engaged John Wood the Elder to re-style the building. Wood added two wings in classic style redolent of his work in Bath, where he designed Queen's Square and the Circus. The barn on the east side of the house, once thought to be of medieval origin, is now believed to have been constructed in the late eighteenth century.

The house remained the property of the Yerbury family until 1903 when John William Yerbury sold it to one Samuel Francis.

Belcombe Court, home of the Yerbury family for nearly two centuries.

Wellclose House

A short distance from Belcombe Court is Wellclose House. Francis's brother Joseph John was living there at the time that Francis was gentrifying the former and it seems likely that John Wood was engaged to re-front the latter. The work was on the pretentious side for a building which was in reality a nice old farmhouse.

The Yerburys were prosperous Bradford clothiers from at least the early seventeenth century. They were also active Presbyterians. Official records show that Francis Yerbury (1638-1720) had his house and a barn (called Kelson's Barn) registered in 1692 as Presbyterian places of worship and that in 1698 Francis Yerbury the Elder and Francis Yerbury the Younger (presumably father and son), with others, were purchasers from Anthony Methuen of land on which to build the Grove Chapel (see above). Joseph John, the one who lived at Wellclose House and re-fronted it, was said by Canon Jones to have been a Quaker but the writer has been unable to confirm this from the records and thinks it unlikely.

Francis (1706-1778), son of the builder of Belcombe Court, trained in London as a barrister but returned to the Bradford clothing business bringing to it a weaving method which he is said to have learned from the silk weavers of Spitalfields. He patented this in 1766 as "a new method of making thin superfine cloth for the summer season at home, and warmer climates abroad, and yet notwithstanding the thinness of the texture, it is more durable than cloth of a greater substance made in the common way." The material came to be known as cassimere (sometimes called kerseymere).

In 1787 Belcombe was the scene of what might have developed into a serious riot. Some 1500 rebellious weavers from Trowbridge marched on Bradford. On arriving at Belcombe Brook they found that John William Yerbury (who had succeeded his father Francis at Belcombe) had mounted two small cannon in the windows to intimidate them. Whether because of the cannon or of John William's eloquence or because Bradford weavers failed to support them, they turned back, their purpose, whatever it was, unaccomplished.

John William Yerbury was one of the sponsors when the Grove Meeting House was belatedly registered as a place of worship in 1793.

BERRYFIELD HOUSE (sometimes called BEARFIELD HOUSE)
The house which has since 1979 been Bradford on Avon hospital, and for some years before that was the maternity hospital, was built in the 1840s (surprisingly given the severe recession) as a clothier's house, probably by Ezekiel Edmonds[9], magistrate and Deputy Lieutenant for the County, who was living there in 1855. Later in the century it was the home of Gerald Augustus Robert Fitzgerald (born 1844) a barrister, son of A O Fitzgerald, Archdeacon of Wells. After that it was the home of Brigadier-General Palmer, a Territorial Army officer who served in the First World War and commanded successively the Royal Wiltshire Yeomanry and the 10th Mounted Brigade. From 1918 to 1922 Brigadier Palmer was Member of Parliament for the Westbury constituency. He died at Bexley, Kent, in 1932.

Berryfield House, now Bradford on Avon Hospital

WOOLLEY GRANGE (formerly WOOLLEY HOUSE)

Built in the late 1600s and owned then by the Baskerville family (members of whom were, incidentally, Quaker clothiers) but later much altered, mainly by Captain Septimus Palairet in 1848 (though he only had it on a 21 year lease) after which he called it Woolley Grange. A further alteration by Palairet was the shifting of the road from Woolley Hamlet to Woolley Green from outside his front door to its present route.

Captain Palairet was a retired army officer who had married an American heiress. During his six years in Bradford (he died in 1854), besides making the changes at Woolley House he paid for the building of Christ Church School and, as we have seen, helped finance the infant rubber industry which his friend Stephen Moulton had just started.

FRANKLEIGH HOUSE,(now THE OLD RIDE PREPARATORY SCHOOL FOR BOYS), Bath Road

Frankleigh House as we see it today was the work of the Bailward family, Quaker clothiers become Methodists become landowners become Anglicans and, by marriage, become landed gentry.

Frankleigh House dates back in part to the early 1600s. The building was restored and extended in 1848 by the three unmarried daughters of Samuel Bailward of Horsington, Elizabeth, Julia and Amelia.

Before that the house had belonged to John Jones (died 1807). Jones had three sons, John, William and Leslie Grove. Son John built the large mill, now Nestle's, at Staverton in 1800 (see above) and became bankrupt in 1813.

Leslie Grove Jones (1779-1839) became in turn sailor, soldier and radical writer. As a teen-age ensign he left the Royal Navy in disgust at what he believed to have been an unjust flogging and joined the army, Lord Lansdowne having obtained for him a commission in the Guards Regiment; in due course he rose to the rank of lieutenant-colonel. He fought in the Peninsular War (1808-1814) and at Waterloo (1815). On leaving the army he dedicated himself to party politics but his political ambitions seem to have been frustrated by lack of funds.

Immediately before John Jones the house was run as a spa by Dr Daniel Jones (no relation) hence, presumably, the later (temporary) style Kingswell Court. (Dr Jones also conducted a spa at Holt, where Sawtell's bedding factory now stands).

After the demise of the Bailward sisters the house became for a while a private "Grammar School" called Kingswell Court, and after that, until his death, the home of Canon the Honourable Sidney Meade (1839-1917), third son of the Earl of Clanwilliam. Canon Meade was for some years a curate of Christ Church, Bradford on Avon.

MIDWAY MANOR and the Shrapnel family

The Shrapnels were Bradford clothiers from at least the seventeenth century. A stone tablet in Holy Trinity church records the deaths of Henry in 1688, three Zachariahs in 1723, 1761 and 1796, the Reverend Joseph in 1821 and General Henry Scrope Shrapnel in 1849.

The Old Manor House of Midway at Wingfield, three miles south of Bradford on the B3109, said to have dated from the twelfth century, was the boyhood home of General Henry Shrapnel, inventor of the exploding shell known by his name. The old house was pulled down and the present one built by Henry Summers Baynton in 1893[10].

General Shrapnel

Henry Scrope Shrapnel was born in Bradford in 1761 and died on 13 March 1842. He was buried in the family vault in Holy Trinity Church. (The year shown on the stone tablet is incorrect; a brass plate in the chancel floor records the correct one). He was the son of the Zachariah Shrapnel who died in 1796.

Henry Shrapnel was a regular officer in the Royal Artillery so keen on improving the efficiency of artillery bombardment that he devoted over many years his own time and money to it. He spent a small fortune on developing his exploding shell over and above what he had spent on designing other devices for increasing fire-power; but his claim for reimbursement from the government fell on deaf ears. even in the light of a despatch from the Waterloo battlefield itself that the shell's deployment for the recapture of the key position at the farmhouse of La Haye Sainte, where the British line had been pierced, had been decisive.

Shrapnel was awarded a pension of £1,200 a year by way of recognition of his services. In the event he would have been better off without it, as he was passed over for promotion and the award was construed in such a way as to nullify other claims he had made for improving fire-power. There was talk of a baronetcy and the king was willing and ready; but Shrapnel seems to have been singularly lacking in friends in high places and nothing came of it. He left the army in 1825 and died at Southampton a very disgruntled man. His son, Henry

General Henry Shrapnel, inventor of the exploding ('shrapnel')
shell. (Photo: Ian Jones, National Army Museum).

Midway Manor, Wingfield

Needham Scrope Shrapnel (1812-1896), after retirement in 1866 made it his business to press his father's claims but met with no greater success. Disenchanted with his native land he went to live in Canada.

On the stone piers of the gateway leading to the house are represented shrapnel shells and the names of battles claimed to have been won by their use: Waterloo, Table Bay, Chuzneemedanse, Kioze, Bidasoa, Tsage and Busaco.

Midway Manor, with some 180 acres, was owned until his death in 1988 by Mr. Timothy Walker. With his wife Rosemary he maintained there a private zoo of rare and exotic animals. Mr. Walker was the United Kingdom chairman of the World Wildlife Fund. At the time of writing the future of the scheme is uncertain but Mrs Walker hopes that it will be possible to continue it in some form.

103

LEIGH HOUSE, now THE LEIGH PARK HOTEL, Bradford Leigh

The house we see today was built in 1820 by Daniel Clutterbuck, a Bradford lawyer, on the site of the sixteenth century property which he had acquired in 1789. Clutterbuck died in 1821 and the estate was sold to Admiral Fellowes. Fellowes (1778-1853), youngest son of Dr William Fellowes, physician to George IV, came to Bradford on retirement after service with the East India Company and the Royal Navy. The next owner (from 1840) was the Reverend John Hopkins Bradney, the rich perpetual curate of Christ Church. After that it belonged to Miss Isabella Poynder, benefactress, as we have seen, of the Christ Church National School. From about 1880 to 1888 the estate was owned by Lady Jane Henrietta Swinburne, whose brother, the poet Charles Algernon Swinburne (1837-1909), is said to have stayed there for a time, and after that by Lord Fitzmaurice of Leigh.

During the Second World War Leigh House became a military hospital. From 1947 it was Bradford on Avon hospital. In 1979, the hospital having moved to Berryfield House, the property was bought by Mr Moody and converted to its present use.

Leigh House, Bradford Leigh, now The Leigh Park Hotel.

Lord Fitzmaürice of Leigh
The most distinguished owner of Leigh House was Edmond George
Petty-Fitmaurice (1846-1935), first Baron Fitzmaurice, second son of
the fourth Marquis of Lansdowne, who lived there from 1890 till his
death.
Fitzmaurice was Liberal Member of Parliament for Calne from 1868 to
1885, and from 1882 to 1885 was Under Secretary of State for Foreign
Affairs in Gladstone's government. He was re-elected to Parliament in
1898 as member for the North Division of Wiltshire. In 1905 he was
elevated to the peerage as Lord Fitmaurice of Leigh, choosing his title
from his home at Bradford Leigh.

Unlike his Tory elder brother, the fifth Marquis, who later became
Viceroy of India, Fitzmaurice was a radical Liberal reformer, concerned
for the underpaid and unenfranchised Wiltshire labouring classes and
particularly interested in educational opportunity for all. It is known
that many a young man in Wiltshire owed his university career to his
unobtrusive generosity. He was a staunch advocate of reform of local
government, land law, licensing law and the House of Lords, and a firm
supporter of Home Rule for Ireland.

II "MADE AL OF STONE"

The streets are narrow and irregular; yet many good houses
present themselves to the eye of the passenger.
The Universal British Directory 1793

Some good ones gone – and some saved
Bradford's charm is perennial. Streets and houses are as enjoyable now
as they ever were. But some buildings that today we should save (often
for fear of what might be put in their place!) have gone long since. At the
corner where the church of St Thomas More (the former town hall) now
stands once stood, as we know from an old print, a most attractive
building; this may have been the inn called The Hare, It was demolished
in 1854 to make way for the present building.

The earlier town hall (or market house as it was usually called) stood at
the foot of Coppice Hill at the eastern end of the Shambles facing what is
now number 32 Silver Street (The Corner Cupboard). Writing in the
Wiltshire Archaeological Magazine in 1881 Canon Jones describes the

building as it had been described to him by a resident who had known it as a boy. According to the Canon's informant:

The Old Market House was originally of what might be termed three storeys. The basement or cellar was on a level with the street opposite the shop now occupied by Mr Budget Jones[11] the entrance joining the Royal Oak, and was used some 60 years ago as a crockery store. The second storey was an open colonnade looking up Coppice Lane and was full of butchers' stalls. The entrance was on the level of the Shambles and the storey itself consisted of three plain round columns one at each angle, between them being wooden palisading and a central column; to this last the ne'er-do-wells who were sentenced for some offence or other to have a whipping were bound. The third or upper storey consisted at one time of a room in which the courts were held and the business of the Manor transacted. But in my time (1820) it was in ruin and the staircase leading to it was gone. I remember, however, that it had three quaint projecting windows of a square-headed form, with thick deeply-moulded oak frames which were filled with small diamond panes of glass and looked into the Old Market Place. I remember the upper part falling down, whilst the lower was still, for some years afterwards, used by the butchers.

Canon Jones observed that against the wall of what was in his day the Royal Oak public house, (that is, the building at the east end of The Shambles on the south side) the lines of the roof gable might still be traced. They still can be. The building, long neglected in the protracted period of recession which, as described elsewhere, had begun around the turn of the century, in 1826 finally collapsed.

Another good building lost by neglect was the Wesleyan Chapel on Coppice Hill; its walls remain to remind us of what it once was. The row of shops in Market Street called Pippet Buildings would certainly have gone the same way and so might the Priory Barn in Newtown and Silver Street House; but all these were saved by the action of Bradford on Avon Preservation Trust.

Through the energy and initiative of the vicar, (the excellent Canon Jones again), St Catherine's Almshouses in Frome Road are still extant, (though probably nothing of the original building remains). The charity

*Where Shambles, Silver Street and Coppice Hill meet was where the old town hall
and market house stood till it collapsed in 1826 for want of maintenance. It served
as a place for public punishment, complete with whipping-post, stock and pillory*

had been well-endowed. In 1702 it had possessed twelve and a half acres.
But in 1834 the Charity Commissioners reported that as a result of gross
misconduct on the part of the trustees more than half the land had
passed to the ownership of either General Shrapnel or Sir John
Hobhouse, with no record of payment. The only accounting the Charity
Commissioners could find was in the banking books of Messrs.
Hobhouse and Co – to whom the charity was in debt. The commissioners found the buildings in a deplorable state and reduced to three
tenements, each of one floor with one almswoman.

In spite of this damning report things went on much as before for the
next 27 years. Then in 1861 the Charity Commissioners, prompted by
Canon Jones, put things on a proper footing. In 1868 the almshouses
were rebuilt (to the design of Bradford architect Charles Adye) as three
new tenements, out of funds (£300) bequeathed by John Bubb. In 1878
the building was enlarged by the trustees to make one more tenement.
Today there are three separate dwellings, two having been combined to

Hall's Almshouses in Frome Road.

108

make one. The trustees are the Lord of the Manor (Sir John Hobhouse), the vicar of Holy Trinity church and two churchwardens.

The Hall's Almshouses[12] in Frome Road, founded in AD 1700 by John Hall, have survived more or less in their original form thanks to benefactors, including the Duke of Kingston and, in the 1890s, Horatio Moulton who repaired and re-roofed them.

III BRADFORD ON AVON PRESERVATION TRUST

The wave of destruction which, triggered by the Housing Act of 1957, swept across the nation in the 1960s came early to Bradford, where the attractive terraces of seventeenth and eighteenth century stone cottages on the north-west slope of the town came under threat.

In December 1957 the Wiltshire Times reported a Bradford Urban District Council proposal to clear Tory, Middle Rank and Newtown of all existing buildings and erect council flats on the site. As a start, 35 houses on Tory and a number on Middle Rank were condemned. Outrage was national as well as local. In Bradford a preservation society (later to be reconstituted as the Bradford on Avon Preservation Trust) was formed with the declared object of maintaining the town's character, architectural interest and scenic qualities and, where new building was necessary, ensuring that it was in keeping.

In June 1963 the national media were able to report the success of the campaign to save the terraces. The local authorities had been won over. Not only had the District Council withdrawn the demolition order to allow a group of ten houses on Tory to be repaired, but the County Council had been a major contributor to the cost of so doing. Fired now with enthusiasm the District Council had purchased cottages on Middle Rank for similar treatment.

Though Bradford was spared the worst excesses of the decade by the energy and dedication of the Preservation Society and its supporters the town was not allowed to go entirely unscathed. The attractive stone-built former Quaker Meeting House which had stood in the town centre since 1718 was demolished and in 1965 a number of agreeable seventeenth century stone houses on St Margaret's Hill were pulled down to make way for council flats for the elderly. Vigorous efforts to secure a reprieve, supported by local and national media, had been in vain.

As time went on the Preservation Society came to be accepted by the authorities as a responsible body whose opinion was worth seeking in

Silver Street House was renovated by Bradford on Avon Preservation Trust in 1977. Left: *The building before rehabilitation,* right: *as it is now.*

Pippett Buildings before and after restoration by Bradford on Avon Preservation Trust in 1982. (Photographs by courtesy of Vernon Gibbs and Partners)

planning matters and so, of more recent years, it has become able to exercise a restraining influence without confrontation. One instance of this was the saving from destruction of the Fitzmaurice Grammar School building in Junction Road after the school joined the Secondary Modern one to form St Laurence Comprehensive School.

The preservationists have not confined themselves to exhortation. To widen its scope the original Preservation Society has been reconstituted as an incorporated charitable body, Bradford on Avon Preservation Trust Ltd. with additional powers, among them the power to acquire property for the purpose of preserving it.

In the late 1960s the then derelict Priory Barn was bought by a member and presented to the Trust, who restored and converted it to its present use as an attractive centre for meetings and small social

Priory Barn, formerly part of the Methuen estate (see page 81), rescued from dereliction by Bradford on Avon Preservation Trust in the 1960s.

THE BUILDINGS

functions. (The architects were Hugh Roberts and Partners). Two other buildings have been rescued from oblivion by the Trust. The late seventeenth century Silver Street House was renovated in 1977 (architect R D Goodall); and the rehabilitation, almost at the point of collapse, of the row of shops in Market Street now called Pippet Buildings, which was completed in 1982, received national acclaim and the 1984 Civic Trust Award. (The architects were Vernon Gibbs and Partners.)

NOTES

1. For a fuller account see Canon J E Jackson's article, reprinted from the Wiltshire Archaeological Magazine on pages 232 to 236 of Canon Jones's History

2. Wiltshire Archaeological Magazine Volume 5 pages 267-341.

3. This was the firm which during the severe industrial recession in 1841 failed and helped precipitate the failure of the bank of Hobhouse, Phillott and Lowder.

4. Mrs Barbara Harvey, a member of Wiltshire Buildings Record, tells me that she has identified the farmhouse called Maplecroft at Frankleigh (ST 823623) as having belonged to Thomas Rogers. Part of this ancient builIding remains as it was in his lifetime, thick walls, heavy joists and a fifteenth century doorway confirming a date of about 1500.

5. John Cam Hobhouse's friendship with the poet Byron was lifelong. Byron drew on the journey that they made together in Albania in his epic poem *Childe Harold; Journey through Albania* is Hobhouse's account. Canto IV of Childe Harold is dedicated to Hobhouse. Hobhouse's *Imitations and Translations from the Ancient and Modern Classics* contains nine poems by Byron.

6. Wiltshire Archaeological Magazine, Volume 41.

7. A coroner or clerk of the market was concerned with enforcement of the weights and measures laws and with fair dealing generally, particularly at markets and fairs. There will have been in Bradford as there was wherever fairs and markets were held, a court of *piedpoudre*. Canon Jones suggested that Pippet Street, the old name for Market Street, got its name from it. It seems likely. Pippet is as near to the French pronunciation as a Wiltshireman might want to get. (In Bristol, where, incidentally, the court, held before a recorder, still survives, they called it piepowder)
   The court of *piedpoudre* was a very minor one, concerned with pedlars and petty chapmen – people with dusty feet. It settled disputes between buyer and seller on the spot; the complaint had to be made on the day the dispute arose and must be settled the same day.

8. Loftie wrote:
   The history of Edward Orpin, who died in his own house at Bradford in 1781 is variously related in the local guide-books, most of them making him the friend of the great artist who was living and painting at number 24 in the Circus at Bath between 1760 and 1774...The truth for once seems to lie with a local tradition, now apparently locally forgotten, but well remembered in 1866, when Mr Wiltshire, the descendant and successor of Gainsborough's friend, died at his house, Shockerwick, in Somersetshire, which lies a short distance east of Bathford on the Corsham Road...It became the

custom, certainly in summer, that the artist should spend the "week's end" with his friend the carrier, Mr Wiltshire, who always refused payment for conveying Gainsborough's pictures to London. On Sunday evenings the parish clerk used to come over the intervening hills in order to read the Bible to the Shockerwick household, and this was probably Gainsborough's sole acquaintance with Orpin, who sat perhaps unwittingly to be immortalised.

I well remember the seven fine pictures, five of which, and among them the portrait of Orpin, hung over the bookcase in the library. Early the following year they were removed to London and sold at Christie's. I was told in the house that they had hung as they were during the auction of the furniture from the time they were painted. The last Mr Wiltshire had lived for many years in great retirement, and nothing had been removed. There were portraits of Foote and Quin the actors, and two of local scenes, gipsies and boys with dogs, besides the two grand landscapes in the joining room, *The Harvest Wagon*, in which there was a portrait of Miss Wiltshire as well as of the artist's daughters, and the *Cattle and Figures* which was also a view in Shockerwick Park... *The Parish Clerk* was bought for the National Gallery for £325 ten shillings...

9. Ezekiel Edmonds, whose mills were in Church Street, was the last clothier member of a family who had been in the business in Bradford since at least 1791. We do not know a great deal about them and it may therefore be of interest to the genealogist or local historian that I chanced upon a descendent of theirs when I was living in the United States of America in the 1960s.
   This was Major General James E Edmonds, a retired officer of the US National Guard, whose great-grandfather James Edmonds enlisted in the Royal Marines at Bradford on Avon on 9 September 1797 and, having served in the Napoleonic Wars, was entitled to a campaign medal but had never claimed it. The story was newsworthy at the time (February 1965) because General Edmonds, working on his family history, had enquired about the medal and was pleasantly surprised to be presented with it; his great-grandfather's entitlement had been confirmed by the Royal Marine Corps Records Office and the Royal Mint had struck one specially for him.

10. According to *Wiltshire and Dorsetshire at the Opening of the 20th Century* published in 1906 in Pike's New Century Series.

11. He meant Budgett & Jones, see note 3 to Chapter 4 on page .

12. We know from the report of an enquiry held on behalf of the Charity Commissioners on 13 February 1901 that those in Hall's Almshouse were rather better off than those in St Catherine's clearly because of the scandalous misapppropriation in the past of the latter's endowment.
   In 1834 three almswomen in St Catherine's were entitled to two shillings and sixpence a week when funds were available. From 1861, when the Charity Commissioners intervened, this was increased to four shillings a week. They were also given five hundredweight of coal at Christmas by a local coal company. The minimum age was 60 and married couples were not allowed.
   The men in Hall's Almshouse were allowed to have their wives with them. In 1834 they were being given three shillings and sixpence a week plus a pair of shoes every year and a coat every second year. In 1901 the weekly allowance was five shillings and they were being allowed two coats a year, one for the summer and one for the winter.

SUGGESTED FURTHER READING

Besides the *Victoria County History* and Canon W H Jones's *Bradford on Avon* the following are suggested for readers with a general interest in Bradford's past:

Langdon, Gee: *The Year of the Map*, Compton Russell, 1976

Niblett, Bertram: *Memories of Bradford on Avon*, Wiltshire Library and Museum Service, 1981

Rawling, Charles: *The Bradford on Avon Pictorial Guide*, 1887

Bradford on Avon: a Pictorial Record, ed. Fassnidge and Maundrell, Wiltshire Library and Museum Service, 1983

Leland's Itinerary in England and Wales Vol I, ed. Toulmin Smith, Centaur Press, 1964

The following books are useful sources of information in their various fields:

Buildings

Nikolaus Pevsner: *The Buildings of England: Wiltshire*, Penguin, rev. ed., 1975

Churches

Wiltshire Meeting House Certificates 1689/1852 ed. John Chandler for the Wiltshire Record Society

The Journal of John Wesley ed. Nehemiah Curnock (8 volumes)

Rawling, Joseph: *The Biographical Records of Joseph Rawling*

Taylor, H M: *J T Irvine's work at Bradford on Avon* reprinted from The Archaeological Journal, Volume 129, for 1972 and published by the Royal Archaeological Institute.

Industry

Mann, J de L: *The Cloth Industry in the West of England from 1640 to 1880*, Alan Sutton, 1987

Ponting, Kenneth: *A History of the West of England Cloth Industry*

Rogers, Kenneth: *Wiltshire and Somerset Woollen Mills*, Pasold Research Fund Ltd, 1976

Rogers, Kenneth: *Warp and Weft: the Somerset and Wiltshire Woollen Industry*, Barracuda Books, 1987

Woodruff, William: *The Rise of the British Rubber Industry during the 19th Century*, Liverpool University

A Guide to the Industrial Archaeology of Wiltshire, ed. M C Corfield, Wiltshire Library and Museum Service, 1978

A TOWN TOUR

The following suggested walk is a fairly comprehensive circular tour which may be taken all at once (an hour to an hour and a half) or in two separate parts, of which part 1 will take three quarters of an hour to an hour.

Part 1   Start at the station car-park. To the south-west, across the railway line, you can see Barton Farm and behind it the medieval tithe barn where our tour will finish. Budbury, where the Iron Age inhabitants and their Roman successors lived is to the north-west of here, roughly where the prominent rectangular building on the skyline (a former rug factory) now stands.

We go out of the car park to St Margaret's Street where facing us is the Old Baptist Chapel and the men's almshouses. Near here stood the medieval leper hospital of St Margaret which gave the locality its name. Walk down St Margaret's Street towards Westbury House. The large building in the car park is St Margaret's Hall. The Quaker meeting house of 1718 and burial ground once occupied the parking area between the hall and the road.

Back in St Margaret's Street, at Westbury House gardens, you are standing where the broad ford was and possibly where Cenwalh fought in AD 652. Cross the road. On the upstream side the town bridge dates back to at least the fourteenth century; the two pointed arches at this end of it are said to be late Norman. From the bridge on the down-river side view the excellent factory building of 1875 and note the small artificial 'island
in the foreground.

Cross the bridge, passing what was once the lock-up or 'blind-house' to what was the old market place; the metal rings set in the parapet on the other side of the bridge were for tethering beasts awaiting sale. Passing the Avon Industrial Polymers factory buildings on the right go a few yards up Silver Street and cross to where Coppice Hill and The Shambles join; this is where the original town hall stood till 1826. Number 6 Silver Street, the building faced with red brick is where John Wesley slept badly: the building is of stone so the brick fronts added around the turn of the present century must have been meant as embellishment.

Further up the hill on the same side is *The Dairy*, part of which dates back to about the fourteenth century. Stroll through The Shambles: the apprently timber-frame buildings are nothing of the kind, they are ancient stone buildings faced with wood and plaster in about the seventeenth century to make them look new.

Across the road on the corner of Market Street and Church Street is the Roman Catholic Church of St Thomas More, built as the town hall). Cross into Church Street and walk about 50 yards to Old Church House (Trinity Church Hall) on the right hand side. The building immediately before it, now a private house, was the Hobhouse, Phillott and Lowder Bank which, disastrously for the town, failed in 1841. Past Old Church House is Druce's Hill House and the houss called the Dutch Barton. On the left is Abbey Mill and in front Abbey House. Ahead is the parish church and to the right the Saxon church. Orpin's House is a few yards ahead on the right and his grave is immediately opposite just over the churchyard wall. In front is the Chantry House.

Go up the narrow footpath past the weavers' cottages called Barton Orchard and up the steps to the street called Newtown. The fountain set in the wall is called Lady Well; this supplied water to cottages and houses in the vicinity before piped water came to the town in 1883. The adjacent fortress-like building, now Long's builder's yard, was the Seven Stars malthouse and brewery. The stream which served Lady Well also served the brewery and powered a waterwheel there which is still in working order (but not accessible to us).

If you do not wish to do the whole tour go back down the steps to Barton Orchard and follow the signpost to the tithe barn. From the tithe barn make your way back to the car park by following the path under the iron railway bridge.

Part 2   From Lady Well take the steep footpath (Well Path) up to Tory. Pause for breath and look out over the town to Westbury Hill and the Westbury White Horse. There, in AD 878, on a barren hillside (in Saxon parlance *ethandune*) King Alfred the Great won the decisive victory over the Danes under Guthrum which we call the Battle of Edington.

Go through the iron gates to visit the chapel of St Mary. Then follow the footpath running round the side of the chapel which leads down

117

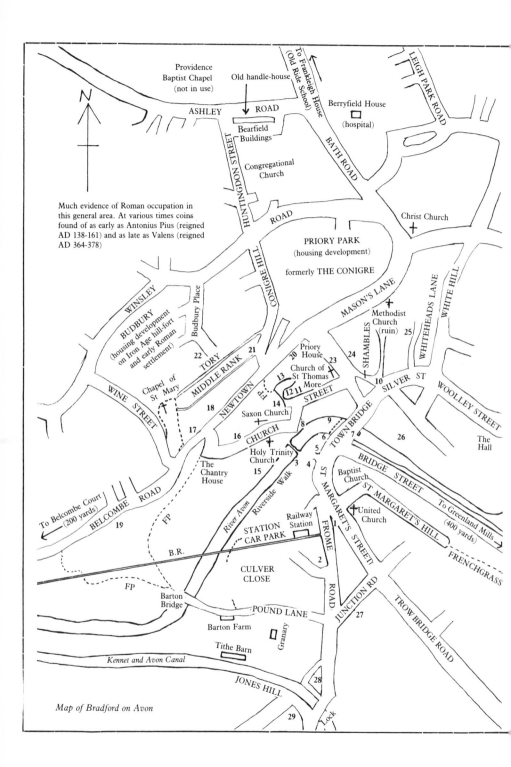

Providence
Baptist Chapel
(not in use)

Old handle-house

To Frankleigh House
(Old Ride School)

Berryfield House

LEIGH PARK ROAD

ASHLEY ROAD

Bearfield
Buildings

Congregational
Church

HUNTINGDON STREET

BATH ROAD

(hospital)

Christ Church

Much evidence of Roman occupation in
this general area. At various times coins
found of as early as Antonius Pius (reigned
AD 138-161) and as late as Valens (reigned
AD 364-378)

ROAD

PRIORY PARK
(housing development)

formerly THE CONIGRE

CONIGRE HILL

MASON'S LANE

WHITEHEADS LANE

WHITE HILL

WINSLEY

BUDBURY
(housing development
on Iron Age hill-fort
and early Roman
settlement)

Budbury Place

Methodist
Church
(ruin) 25

SHAMBLES

SILVER ST

TORY

MIDDLE RANK

22

21

Priory
House

20

23

24

10

WOOLLEY STREET

Chapel of
St Mary

NEWTOWN

Church of
St Thomas
More

13

STREET

12 11

WINE STREET

18

14

Saxon Church

8

9

TOWN BRIDGE

26

The
Hall

17

16

CHURCH

Holy Trinity
Church

15

6

5

7

BRIDGE STREET

ST MARGARET'S HILL

To Greenland Mills
(400 yards)

The
Chantry
House

River Avon

Riverside Walk

3

4

ST MARGARET'S STREET

Baptist
Church

FRENCHGRASS

To Belcombe Court
(200 yards)

BELCOMBE ROAD

19

FP

United
Church

Railway
Station

STATION
CAR PARK

FROME ROAD

JUNCTION RD

27

TROWBRIDGE ROAD

B.R.

2

FP

CULVER
CLOSE

Barton
Bridge

POUND LANE

Barton Farm

Granary

Tithe Barn

Kennet and Avon Canal

JONES HILL

28

Map of Bradford on Avon

29

Lock

Key to Map:

1 Hall's Charity almshouses for men.
2 Probable site of St Margaret's leper hospital (medieval).
3 St Margaret's Hall (one-time dye-house).
4 Site of 1718 Quaker Meeting House and burial ground.
5 Westbury House.
6 Former ford, probably the historic 'broad ford'.
7 Former blindhouse or lock-up (so-called chapel).
8 Abbey Mills
9 Remains of former platform in the river for washing wool.
10 Site of earliest town hall.
11 Church House.
12 Trinity Church Hall and Freemasons' Lodge.
13 Druce's Hill House.
14 Abbey House, Abbey Yard and Dutch Barton.
15 Kingston Place (former vicarage).
16 Orpin's House.
17 Lady Well.
18 Former Seven Stars Brewery and Malthouse.
19 Wellclose House.
20 Priory Barn.
21 Grove Meeting House.
22 Budbury House (former rug factory).
23 Pippet Buildings.
24 Town Club, site of Maidenhead Inn and former Methodist chapel.
25 Quaker Meeting House.
26 Site of Kingston Mill.
27 Former Fitzmaurice Grammar School building.
28 St Catherine's almshouses for women.
29 Kennet and Avon Canal wharf.

Wine Street, turn left and at the junction with Newtown turn right. This is Belcombe Road. Opposite the road called Belcombe Place is Wellclose House; the upper part of the John Wood frontage can be seen over the wall.

Continue along Belcombe Road about 400 yards for Belcombe Court on the right. Retrace steps for about 200 yards, cross the road, take the footpath down to and over the railway line and head for Barton Farm and the tithe barn. The Kennet and Avon Canal runs behind the barn, with the canal lock and wharf about a hundred yards away. From the tithe barn and Barton Farmhouse return to the station car park by following the path under the iron railway bridge.

The Shambles

In Newtown, new *in late seventeenth century days of industrial revival.*

Lumbering Saxon ox-wagons beat out the track to and from the river – crossing to form what we call Silver Street. The building-line is, at latest, medieval.

The street now called Market Street was formerly Pippet(t) Street from the junction with the market place at the bridge foot. See page 113, note 7 for possible reason for the name Pippet.

Hang-dog Alley led from Church Street to the bull-pit

Old Bank House in Church Street was Joseph Rawling's printing press and stationer's shop from 1820 (see page 95).

Cottages in Church Street. They are believed to have been built over the graveyard of the Saxon Church.

The newly-created Riverside Walk.

SOME BRADFORD ON AVON PLACE NAMES AND THEIR ORIGINS

Barton Farm, Barton Orchard and Dutch Barton

The word barton, which occurs frequently in English place-names, derives from Anglo-Saxon *beretum*, *bere* being barley and *tum* an enclosure. The term has been used variously down the ages, sometimes to mean not just a field of barley but also a farmyard and even a manor house. In Wessex it usually denoted a great farm; a small one was called a living.

Bearfied and Berryfield

More likely to have been a barley field than one where there were bears or berries. *Bere* was Anglo-Saxon for barley, see above.

Budbury

English place-names with *bury* (Anglo-Saxon *burg* or *burh*) often denote a Roman or other pre-English fort and this is the case here. Canon Jones suggested that the name Budbury might derive from the presence of a chapel (St Mary, Tory), the element *bud* perhaps a corruption of Anglo-Saxon *bed* a prayer. Another suggestion has been that it was the site of a settlement of a Saxon chieftain called Budda.

Bull Pit

This street-name reminds us of the once very popular entertainment of setting dogs to attack a bull tied to a stake. In 1835 in the face of strong resistance, an Act of Parliament made it illegal.

Conigre Hill

The word conigre is Wessex dialect for a rabbit warren. Rabbits were encouraged to colonise. They were the poor man's equivalent of the rich man's ice-house, a valuable source of protein at any time and an aid to survival in the life-threatening winter months. (Readers familiar with Richard Adams's *Watership Down* will remember how, in their wanderings, the rabbits came upon one and but for the instinctive misgivings of Fiver and the mishap which befell Bigwig would have joined it). But in some cases they were maintained as game preserves, with shooting for sport from November to January. Such will have been the two Bradford conigres shown on the 1841 tithe map; Great Conigre which was part of the Priory estate, belonging at the time to Thomas Hosier Saunders, and Little Conigre which belonged to Thomas Wheeler. Great Conigre occupied what is now called Priory Park and the name of the lane leading steeply up from Newtown remains to remind us of it; Little Conigre was the part of Budbury lying behind the eastern end of Tory.

BRADFORD ON AVON PAST AND PRESENT

Culver Close

This is another reminder of medieval Bradford, recalling that hereabouts there was once a pigeon-house or dovecot belonging to Barton Farm. The word derives from Anglo-Saxon *culfre* meaning a dove or pigeon. The building will have been significant; in the Middle Ages only the Lord of the Manor or the parson was allowed to have one. This prerogative lapsed with the passage of time and by the sixteenth century it was established that any freeholder might have a dovecote on his land. Older Bradford houses will often be found to have recesses built into a wall to house a small flock of pigeons, which, like the wild rabbits enticed into the conigre (see above), made for a valuable and economical supplement to diet.

Frenchgrass

Frenchgrass is another name for sainfoin *(onobrychis sativa)*. It thrives on light, dry, calcareous soil and hence does well here. It is particularly suitable for grazing sheep. Frenchgrass was at one time the name of a large pasture on the north-east side of Trowbridge Road; nothing now remains of it but the lane which bears its name.

Huntingdon Street

Named after the chapel of the religious denomination called the Countess of Huntingdon's Connexion, an offshoot of Wesleyan Methodism, see page 56 .

St Margaret's Street, St Margaret's Hill, etc.

Named after the leper hospital of St Margaret, see page 23 .

Newtown

The street called Newtown was 'new' in the late 1600s when it was a development (on land owned by the Methuen family) on the edge of the 'old town.' Workers from elsewhere will have been attracted to Bradford by the prospect of employment in the once more thriving clothing industry.

Pound Lane

Poundagium was the right or duty of impounding straying cattle, a term which included horses, sheep and other domestic animals. The pound was where they were held. Once impounded they were in the custody of the law and could only be retrieved on payment of a penalty plus compensation for any damage done. Like most country towns Bradford had a pound.

The Shambles

This little shopping street gets its name from the Anglo-Saxon word *scamel,* meaning a small bench or stool on which goods were exposed for sale. The goods displayed were usually meat and a shambles came to be in effect, a meat-market. It is probable that Bradfordians have shopped here for more than a thousand years.

Silver Street

There are streets so named in many Wiltshire towns besides Bradford. They are to be found in Calne, Malmesbury, Potterne, Salisbury, Trowbridge, Warminster and Wilton. As they are always in the centre they are where money changed hands a good deal. Bradford's Silver Street was not always so named. According to Canon Jones★ it was formerly Fox Street and Gregory Street. The section leading from the town bridge was at one time called Old Market Place.

Tory and Tory Place

The name Tory derives from Anglo-Saxon *torr* meaning a high rocky place.

Woolley Street

Canon Jones tells us that a chapel dedicated to St Olave once stood at the corner of the lane leading to White Hill. St Olave Street became Tooley Street and by Jones's time Woolley Street.

Many street-names derive from the presence of a family prominent locally in their day but now long forgotten. Such are Druce's Hill, Jones Hill, Kingston Road (formerly Frogmere Street, renamed in honour of the Duke of Kingston), Morgan Hill (before 1724 St Margaret's Hill and now St Margaret's Hill again), Whiteheads Lane, and White Hill. Some of these eponymous street-names have been lost: St Margaret's Place was Bush's Alley, leading from Beasor Street (which formed part of St Margaret's Street). Some streets have changed their locations: Old Market has become part of Silver Street and what is now called Market street was formerly Pippet Street. Some names and ways have fallen into disuse: Hang-dog Alley used to join Bull Pit and Church Street, though this has recently been re-opened by the present owners as a permissive path during daylight hours on week days. Some names have been lost: Pando Street, Alto (or High) Street and Elbridge Lane (probably deriving its name, as the town of Elbridge in Kent does, from Anglo-Saxon *thelbrycg,* a plank bridge, and suggesting the possibility that the Saxons had some sort of rudimentary bridge across the river.)

★Article in the Wiltshire Archaeological Magazine Vol.XX pages 306-322

INDEX

Abbey House 29,79
Abbey Mill **30**,33,35
Adam le Folur 27,28
Adye, Charles, architect 107
Aerosol gaskets and seals 36
Aethelred the Unredy, King of Wessex
  14,15,16
Agaric Ltd 39
Agnes de Aula 50
Aldhelm 14,45,48
Angels, stone carvings of in Saxon church
  44,47
Anstie Ltd 40
Aubrey, John (1626-1697) 65,(note 11)
Avon Industrial Polymers 10,35
Avon Rubber Company 35
Avonside Iron Foundry 37
Awdry, Sir John, trustee of Saxon church 45

Bailward, Amelia 100
Bailward, Anne 60,63
Bailward, Constant (born Owen) 58,63,64-65
  (note 9)
Bailward, Elizabeth 100
Bailward family 91,100
Bailward, John (I) 63
Bailward, John (II) 63
Bailward, Julia 100
Bailward, Samuel 63,100
"Ballard" (Bailward), Mrs 64 (note 9)
Bank, Hobhouse, Phillott and Lowder, failure
  of 86
Baptist Chapel, Old 54
Baptists 53
Baptists, Particular (Zion Baptists) 55
Barnwell, E L, trustee of Saxon church 45
Barton Bridge **22**
Barton Farm 18,22
Baskerville family 100
Baskerville, John 63
Baynton, Rachel (born 1695) 78
Baynton, Thomas and Elizabeth 78
Bearfield Congregational Church 56,57
Beddoe, John 81,84,86
Beer and Methodism 65 (note 10)
Belcombe Court **96**
Bellatt, Richard 25
Bellcombe Brook House – see Belcombe Court

Berryfield (or Bearfield) House 51,**99**,104
Bethel Chapel 56
Bethell House – see Westbury House
Bethell, Dr 88
Bethell Quarry 39
Bethell, Richard (1800-1873) 1st Lord West-
  bury 88
Bethell, Richard and John, maltsters 37
Bidgood, Mr 62
Bird, William, vicar and chantry priest 25,48
Bishop's Bible 50,64(note 2)
Blackmore, Richard, maltster 37
Blake, Miss, head mistress of Fitzmaurice
  Grammar School 74
Blenheim, Battle of 26,43 (note 2)
Blindhouse **59**,65 (note 11)
Bradford on Avon Hospital 99,104
Bradford on Avon Preservation Trust 106,109
Bradford on Avon Town Club – see Town
  Club
Bradford on Avon Urban District Council 109
Bradney, Rev. John Hopkins 51,104
Brewer, William 29
Brewing – see brewing and malting
Bridge, Norman 16,**59**
Brierley, S J, mechanical engineers 37
British and Foreign School Society 69
British Schools 51,69,71,72
Broad ford, the 12,**13**
Brown, Ebenezer (fl 1807) 84
Broome, John, early Baptist 54
Broughton, Baron – see Hobhouse, Sir John
  Cam
Brown, William 62
Bruce, The Hon W N 69
Brunel 43
Bryant, Caleb 71
Bryant, Mercy 71
Bubb, John 67,107
Buchholz relay 39
Budbury 11
Budgett and Jones 64 (note 3), 114 (note 11)
Budgett, James 51,64 (note 3),106
Butt, John Thornton 68
Bull Pit Mill 33
Byron, James M 62
Byron, Lord 113 (note 5),86

130

BRADFORD ON AVON PAST AND PRESENT

More books from Ex Libris Press are described below: